SCOTLAND'S HOUSING

EXPO 2010

ISBN: 978-1-905061-28-0

Published by A+DS (Architecture and Design Scotland)

http://www.ads.org.uk/

This document is also available on the Scottish Government website:
www.scotland.gov.uk

APS Group Scotland
DPPAS11056 (03/11)

FOREWORD

The Highland Council and the Highland Housing Alliance are to be congratulated on what they have achieved with Scotland's first Housing Expo project.

Although the economic recession and the worst winter for 30 years made what was always an ambitious project much more difficult to deliver, the Expo was able to open on time because of the tremendous efforts made on site by the Highland Housing Alliance, the builders and the design teams. I visited the project with the First Minister less than a week before the Expo opened and I am well aware of the efforts that were being made at that time and which Susan Torrance refers to in her chapter.

The Expo was the first project of its kind in this country, inspired by the successful Finnish Housing Fairs which take place every year in Finland. The aim of the Expo was to showcase innovative, sustainable housing and placemaking to a wide audience and in doing so to help change attitudes towards house and place design. The Expo goes a long way to demonstrate that by designing carefully for the specific site conditions, and making good use of what nature gives us, we can make much progress towards our objectives of reducing energy use in our housing.

But the event itself is only one part of the Expo story. An important characteristic of the project is that it is a permanent example of what we can achieve when we start to think more radically about housing design and layout. We hope that the Expo will be seen by local authorities throughout Scotland as a helpful exemplar of what is achievable in terms of site layout and placemaking, as well as in terms of individual house design.

Works on site at Milton of Leys are now completed and as the occupants of the Expo houses begin to move into their new homes, we are thinking about what we will be able to learn from their experiences and how we can evaluate the success of the project in the longer term. We hope to carry out a monitoring exercise of the houses in use, to see just how energy-efficient they are and what their occupants come to think about the innovative features in the longer term.

We have commissioned this book because we are keen to record the achievements of the Expo project and want to involve a wider audience in the debate about what was demonstrated by the project. This is, of course, part of the wider debate on how we should design housing and how we should live in the first part of the 21st century and that is why we have made the Expo one of the exemplar case studies in **Homes fit for the 21st Century** the Scottish Government's vision for housing in the next decade, which we launched in February.

We are living in a period where we are having to make rapid adjustments to take account of climate change and the depletion of fossil fuels. The Building Standards which set minimum standards for the design of new buildings have now entered into a period of step changes which will progressively require new buildings to be more energy efficient in terms of the net production of carbon dioxide created by their use. Many of the houses at the Expo site demonstrate how we can design to achieve more energy efficient housing and are a useful staging post for helping us decide how to build the future.

This book records the story of the Expo so far. I hope you are inspired by it.

Alex Neil:
Minister for Housing and Communities

FIGURE 1.1

FIGURE 1.2

FIGURE 1.4

FIGURE 1.3

FIGURE 1.5

INTRODUCTION TO THE EXPO STORY

" Scotland's first Housing Expo was made possible by the determined actions of a number of individuals all of whom had a belief that it was a truly worthwhile development."

FIGURE 1.6

THE EXPO STORY

Scotland's Housing Expo in 2010 was the first of its kind in Scotland and the UK. It was based on similar projects found across mainland Europe, and the Finnish Housing Fair in particular, where the concept has grown in popularity over a number of years. If we believe the key to success of any project is in the planning, then a great part of the appeal of Scotland's first ever Housing Expo must be credited to the masterplan, (prepared by Cadell2, urban designers and architects). The composition they created, of terrace, avenue, square and a village green creates a real feeling of community and a sense of place.

In 2007 a competition to design homes for specific sites within a masterplan drew considerable interest from architects across Scotland. The competition, accredited by the Royal Incorporation of Architects in Scotland (RIAS) attracted 88 high quality entries. At that time it was hoped that the Expo would be completed and open to the public in August 2009, appropriately Scotland's "Year of Homecoming". All of this would have been realised had it not been for the detrimental effects of the recession in terms of stalling investment in house building just at the time when the first turf was due to be cut. For the first time, completing Scotland's first ever Housing Expo, seemed impossible.

The Highland Housing Alliance (HHA), the development company owned by the five Highland based housing associations, two housing trusts and The Highland Council, was charged with the responsibility of delivering the completed housing development. However, work could not begin without securing funding in the first instance. The deadline was drawing closer, and we all – the Board, architects, developers and contractors – realised that if we were ever to see the completion of a Housing Fair, then we would have to re-think our plans. So the Board agreed to buy more time by postponing the event until August 2010.

It is at this point I believe, that recognition must be given to those who worked for The Scottish Government in Housing Investment and Architecture and Place: this was never seen as an easy project to bring to fruition and without a number of individuals seeing the potential and working together it would have remained forever on the drawing board. The Highland Council, through the Planning and Development and Housing departments supported the Expo's Advisory Board and Board, who tried to articulate the detail of the process and deliver, what we by now believed to be an essential development. No longer just a nice thing to do, but a necessity. The Highland Housing Alliance was charged with arranging the finance, negotiating with six Highland contractors and bridging the public and private house building sectors. The Housing and Communities Minister, Alex Neil, recognised the worth of the project and gave his personal and The Scottish Government's support.

The months passed and the new deadline of August 2010 should have seen early May 2009 as the new start date. But in reality it wasn't until November 2009 that all of the component parts were in place to allow this to happen and there followed an unbelievably tight programme of work. Well do I remember a seminal moment when asking Susan Torrance of the HHA if it really was possible to complete what should have been a fifteen month work schedule, in less than eight. Her response was positive, with the proviso of a mild winter to allow for an intensive building programme. Milton of Leys, the selected site of the Expo, which sat above the snow-line, suffered even more than the rest of Scotland, in the worst winter in 30 years.

Throughout the following seven months we, the Expo Board, experienced more highs and lows than a snakes and ladders board. The risk register showed many greens, a few ambers and terrifyingly, one or two persistent reds. The days lengthened, the snow disappeared, the shapes and forms of houses miraculously appeared. Scotland's Housing Expo was indeed to become a reality.

The First Minister and the Minister for Housing and Communities visited the site five days before we were to be open to the public. Rain had turned the whole place into a quagmire. heavy plant lumbered its way determinedly criss-crossing our paths as we walked in

FIGURE 1.7

FIGURE 1.8

yellow jackets, hard hats and steel-toed wellies around the site. I understand that over five hundred people were working on the site that day, and indeed until the wee hours on the eve of opening. The feeling of anxiety did not show as we talked our way around the site explaining some of its special features. The Highland Housing Alliance and their contractors had pulled the proverbial rabbit out of the hat. We would indeed have a housing Expo of which the nation could be proud. Both Ministers seemed impressed and if they had any doubts, they didn't voice them.

" The creative industries offer a rich seam in which Scotland should invest and the Expo shone a light on some of what we can do when given the opportunity."

The 1st of August, 2010 is a day that few of us connected with the Expo are ever likely to forget. The pipe-band played, the café was open and the coffee was good, but best of all, there was a queue forming at 9.30am on a dreich Sunday morning eagerly waiting to see what the Expo was all about.

And what was it all about? It was about promoting new ideas in architecture, it was about sustainable living in terms of the energy we use or re-use, it was about living in an urban setting, designed to give the residents the space both inside and outside for comfortable living in the 21st century. The innovative designs were clearly controversial in the best possible way. Conversations and debates about likes and dislikes, good design and planning, were heard in the houses and in the café as personal observations and opinions were expressed. The Expo was working.

At the end of the first day, of the 700 people who attended, many swapped their single visit ticket for a monthly multi-pass when they realised there was more to see than an hour or two would allow.

The Board of the Expo having cranked up the Expo engine, were very much hanging on to the back bumper as the development took shape. Staff within the Council gave a great deal of their time and expertise to put what became known as the Event around the core business of the houses. This made the Expo child friendly (children went free) with several activities in a few of the houses: modelling their own Expo houses in clay in one or building Lego masterpieces in another.

The café was, as it should be, the social hub of the Expo. The artists and craftsmen and agencies who occupied the houses with exhibitions and technical displays contributed to the overall satisfaction of the visitor. And each house 'ambassador' took pride in explaining the nuances of 'their house' to members of the public and professionals alike.

I'm sure that the architects, builders and other professionals involved and visiting will have their experiences recorded elsewhere in this publication. I would like to especially refer to the seminars organised by Sust., Architecture and Design Scotland's Sustainability in Architecture Programme. (Ref 1.1). While these seminars were directed mostly at the industry, they did attract a number of lay visitors too. Topics included planning issues, new building techniques, climate change and its effects, recycling, low energy design, renewable energy systems, education in architecture, new building standards, energy labelling and use of local materials, among many others.

There are many outcomes from the Expo and a great deal was learned. It is hoped that this programme of seminars might be replicated across Scotland to the benefit of everyone. The passionate speakers who contributed, all expert in their field, have a great deal to offer in this brave new world of future house building in Scotland and we must make best use of their talents.

In summary, Scotland has many notable architects whose work is not as widely known or promoted as it should be. The creative industries offer a rich seam in which Scotland should invest and the Expo shone a light on some of what we can do when given the opportunity. The final analysis of this project will undoubtedly give confidence to all of the agencies and sponsors, local authorities, planning and development departments, private and social housing developers and politicians, that this first Expo, in spite of all the difficulties that it had to over-come, should be the first of many.

The Board of the Expo and our Principal Partners made invaluable financial and in-kind contributions, without which this event would never have happened. Their enthusiasm never waned and we are deeply indebted to them for their unfaltering support (Ref 1.2).

Scotland's first Housing Expo was made possible by the determined actions of a number of individuals all of whom had a belief that it was a truly worthwhile development. The attendance of over 34,000 people is proof that there is enormous potential to make a start on the next one.

Jean Urquhart
Chair of the Expo Board

THE EXPO IDEA

" The idea of a Scottish Housing Expo
has its origins in the Nordic Countries,
where historically the concept has
proven very successful in stimulating
high quality design and innovation in
mainstream housing."

FIGURE 2.1 FINNISH HOUSING FAIR, ESPOO 2006

CHAPTER 2

INTRODUCTION

Scotland has a history of involvement in design festivals dating from as far back as the Empire Exhibition of 1938, which took place in Bellahouston Park in Glasgow, to The Glasgow Garden Festival in 1988, Homes for the Future in 1999, and Glasgow 1999 – UK City of Architecture and Design.

The idea of a Scottish Housing Expo has its origins in visits to the Nordic Countries, where historically the concept has proven very successful in stimulating high quality design and innovation in mainstream housing. Finland in particular has refined the concept over the last 40 years, and Scotland's Housing Expo is based upon the Finnish Housing Fair model. The initial concept was particularly influenced by the Oulu Fair of 2005.

The majority of the housing currently built for private occupation in Scotland is produced by developers, almost exclusively on a speculative build nature and with practically no input to the design by the purchaser or occupants. Around 70% of this is built using timber frame, which is almost exclusively manufactured from imported softwood. By contrast, most new and improved homes funded by The Scottish Government, for affordable rent, are likely to have had design input from an architect, with the commissioning housing association acting as client on behalf of the occupants. Greater attention is also liable to have been paid to wider sustainability issues by this sector due to funding conditions in relation to meeting Government targets. Design and sustainability issues are often also important considerations in the design of the small number of self-build homes started in Scotland each year.

In recognition of a need to raise the bar in terms of design quality within Scotland's built environment, particularly housing, the aim of Scotland's first Housing Expo in Inverness in 2010 was to give a national focus to key issues of importance to The Scottish Government. These ranged from the development of low carbon design strategies to the complementary roles of design and sustainability within both public and private housing and a demonstration of how Scotland's built environment could look in the future.

The objectives were:

- to showcase innovative, sustainable housing and placemaking to a wide audience and to help change attitudes towards house and place design;

- to stimulate the construction industry in terms of consideration of design-led housing solutions and high quality home-grown and manufactured skills, materials and products;

- to investigate and trial new ways of thinking about places, design and materials.

Visits to Housing Fairs and Expos in other parts of Europe highlighted an opportunity to demonstrate how the occupant can become involved in the design process, including influencing house layout and fabric choices, and bringing individual needs more into focus in future design developments. This would allow the prospective occupant to engage directly with the house-builder, and could ultimately positively increase demand for home grown products and services.

FIGURE 2.2 FINNISH HOUSING FAIR, HEINOLA 2004

BACKGROUND

The original idea for the first Housing Fair in Scotland, or Scotland's Housing Expo as it became known, grew out of a study tour to the 2004 Finnish Housing Fair in Heinola, organised by the Forestry Commission Scotland and Highland Birchwoods and which included officials from The Highland Council and the then Scottish Executive (now The Scottish Government). Following this visit, The Highland Council developed the idea of the Housing Expo in association with other interested organisations, Highland Council officials and elected representatives attended study tours to Finnish Housing Fairs in the three following years at Oulu, Espoo and Hämeenlinna.

In parallel with these subsequent trips, the Scottish Executive commissioned a desktop study to explore other similar models throughout Europe.

Of the Housing Fairs and Expos researched, no two were the same, however, there was much to be learned from what had gone before. One factor that had to be considered was the extent to which the UK construction climate differs from that of the Nordic and other European countries, where sustainability and low energy design are mainstream activities. In addition, attitude to home ownership differs across Europe. Whilst on the one hand in the UK we do not (necessarily) tend to think of a home as being for life, on the other hand, home ownership tends to be higher in the UK than in other parts of mainland Europe.

The study concluded that the Scottish Executive was unlikely to be in a position to provide full financial support for such an event, however some support from government, in the form of start-up funding seemed possible. It also identified opportunities to encourage 'design innovation', through an Expo. For example, the inclusion of novel construction techniques and novel renewable energy systems.

FINNISH HOUSING FAIRS

The Finnish fairs have been held in a different
municipality each year since 1970 and are
an annual event, consisting of permanent
developments on masterplanned sites,
with a series of plots containing one or
more dwellings, designed and constructed
by different designer/constructor teams.
Responsibility for planning, constructing
and holding each event lies jointly with the
Finnish Housing Fair Co-operative (Suomen
Asuntomessut (Ref 2.1)) and the municipality
that has been selected by a competitive process
to hold the fair in that year. The Housing Fair
Co-operative was initially funded by a number
of Finnish banks, who remain board members
of the organisation, but it no longer receives
any external funding. The Co-operative has,
however, accumulated funds of around €5m,
which it uses as up-front funding for the
events and which is fully recovered through a
share of ticket sales, sponsorship and income
from exhibition space taken up by commercial
organisations represented at the fairs.

In Finnish Housing Fairs, the vast majority
of houses are built by local companies, using
a variety of building and cladding materials,
usually sourced from local or regional suppliers
in Finland, including wood in particular. The
Fair is open to the public each day for one
month between mid July and mid August and is
the largest summer event in Finland, attracting
up to 200,000 visitors. There is intense
competition amongst local authorities to
host the next event.

FIGURE 2.3 FINNISH HOUSING FAIR, ESPOO 2006

" The Finnish Fair is seen as a major
opportunity for developers to show
off the quality of their design and
build capabilities, and to discuss with
prospective clients what they can do
for them."

FIGURE 2.4 FINNISH HOUSING FAIR, ESPOO 2006

FIGURE 2.6 FINNISH HOUSING FAIR, ESPOO 2006

FIGURE 2.5 FINNISH HOUSING FAIR, HAMEENLINNA 2007

FIGURE 2.7 FINNISH HOUSING FAIR, ESPOO 2006

FIGURE 2.8 FINNISH HOUSING FAIR, ESPOO 2006

The Finnish Fair features a variety of building systems, as well as the many different house designs. It is seen as a major opportunity for developers to show off the quality of their design and build capabilities, to promote the range of products they offer, and to discuss with prospective clients what they can do for them.

Each fair is developed and delivered on a not for profit basis by the Finnish Housing Fair Co-operative. The criteria used to select the host location include the need for additional housing in a particular municipality. Once selected, the local authority develops a masterplan, encompassing the number, size and layout of individual house plot and a theme they wish to see addressed in the proposed development. The scale of fairs varies, but recent events have been of the order of 40 - 60 units, with circa 20-30% of the units built as affordable rental properties (local authority or privately owned) and 70-80% for owner occupation. These latter were designed in conjunction with, and built for, a specific client family or a client architect. Generally, the Housing Fair Co-operative seeks to build fair developments where 10% of the houses are controversial in design terms, 30% aim to be something that most people have not seen before and 60% are good examples of current design practice for the general public to see.

The size and location of each serviced plot determines the fixed price. The municipality then seeks design proposals for each plot, and at this stage the competition is not based on price offered per plot but on the perceived quality of the house design.

Planning guidelines are given at the outset, with the local planning authority having a strong input to each proposal as well as retaining the final decision on what is acceptable. Within the basic rules they do however permit a considerable degree of design flexibility.

Costs include site purchase and servicing, project management, promotion and running the event. Sources of income include: ticket and programme sales, fees from exhibitors, central government finance, some EU finance towards some specific elements, sponsorship and plot sales.

From visiting the Finnish Fairs, it was evident that there was a clear benefit from the presence of the co-operative as an umbrella organisation to take on the organisation of these housing fairs in the long term, thus developing experience over the years to help ensure that a consistently high quality of product is on offer.

FIGURE 2.9 FINNISH HOUSING FAIR, ESPOO 2006

Housing Fair developments are linked with, and integrated into, the wider local community, by a variety of means, and are not simply stand alone curiosity sites. Families move into the homes almost immediately after the event. Over time, the sites transform well from a major tourist attraction to a small local community.

Of all the options studied, the Finnish Housing Fairs seemed to offer a model of the most appropriate scale to form the basis of a Scottish event.

Finland has a similar population size and spread to that of Scotland and a similar contrast of big cities and rural communities.

The appropriateness of adopting a tried and tested model lies in the fact that it limits the risk for the organisers, in that it is based on a managed/supported developer/architect partnership, decided by competition. However, it was noted that adopting the Finnish model could lead to up to 30 different house types on the site, which although difficult to manage, might lead to a more radical outcome. Potential logistical problems were also raised with regard to placemaking and planning generally, but it was thought that this could be controlled via the masterplanning exercise and through good management of the process. And so it was decided that this approach should be retained as an ultimate goal, while acknowledging that it might be difficult to achieve for a first event, where a more pragmatic approach might be necessary with say, three small areas or 'streets' of around 50 dwellings, with a few 'special' houses that explore specific issues in detail.

FIGURE 2.10 FINNISH HOUSING FAIR, HAMEENLINNA 2007

Specifically, it was anticipated that in a Scottish Housing Fair, the overarching theme would be **'sustainability'**, and that within this general theme, the key factors relating to this, such as sustainable urban planning, client consultation, healthy materials, energy and resources, healthy lifestyles, etc., would be explored.
Ideas around this included:
- the acoustic house
- the solar house
- the flexible house
- the zero energy house
- the zero CO_2 house
- the recycled house
- the all wooden house
- the healthy house
- the prefabricated house.

Lori McElroy

THE EXPO COMPETITION

" The process of developing the
masterplan commenced with
design-orientated research into
Highland settlement patterns and
the local landscape."

FIGURE 3.1

CHAPTER 3

BACKGROUND TO THE COMPETITION

Cadell2 were appointed by the Highland Housing Alliance as Masterplan Lead Consultant in mid October 2006. We assisted with the assembly of an infrastructure design team including Martin Stockley Associates as Streetscape Engineer, Max Fordham and Partners as M&E and sustainability consultants, WSD (Scotland) as Valuer and Quantity Surveyor and W.A. Fairhurst and Partners as infrastructure Services Engineers.

A comprehensive masterplanning process guided the housing of the Expo, involving work with the winning architects, the local community and other stakeholders. The first step in delivering the Expo was the development of the Framework document that formed the brief for the Expo Design Competition, which was run by the Royal Incorporation of Architects in Scotland (RIAS) in 2007 [Figure 3.2]. Cadell2 led the infrastructure design team, and designed the site layout, public spaces and streets of the Expo as part of our role. Design Coding formed a benchmark for the architecture, maintaining design integrity during implementation. The masterplan also addressed planning policy, prioritising issues of placemaking, community planning and sustainable development. Latterly we were given a design co-ordination role for the interfaces between the 27 individual plot design teams and the infrastructure design team, during RIBA Stages D and E (the Design Development to Detailed Planning stage and Preparation of Technical Design and Specifications of the Design).

The choice of site, means of implementation and timescale were established by the Expo Advisory Board prior to our appointment. Whilst the Balvonie site was recognised as being less than ideal, due to its remoteness from central Inverness, there were mitigating factors including planned transport links, services and a nearby local centre. Importantly the site was considered to have the advantages of being serviceable and developable within the original timescale of August 2009.

The Advisory Board had established that the Highland Housing Alliance would take the lead in managing delivery of the housing, supported by The Highland Council. The housing was to be procured in plots either, for affordable homes, through Housing Associations or, for private houses, by individual plot teams who would purchase and build out their plots. In both cases it was intended that teams would be selected through the vehicle of a design competition in early 2007, to be managed by the RIAS. A bid element was avoided by fixing plot purchase values at the outset. Plot developers were desirable but not mandatory. The build cost would be in the control of each plot development team.

The timescale was established consistent with holding an event in August 2009 to coincide with Scotland's Year of Homecoming.

FIGURE 3.2 AERIAL SKETCH OF EXPO SITE

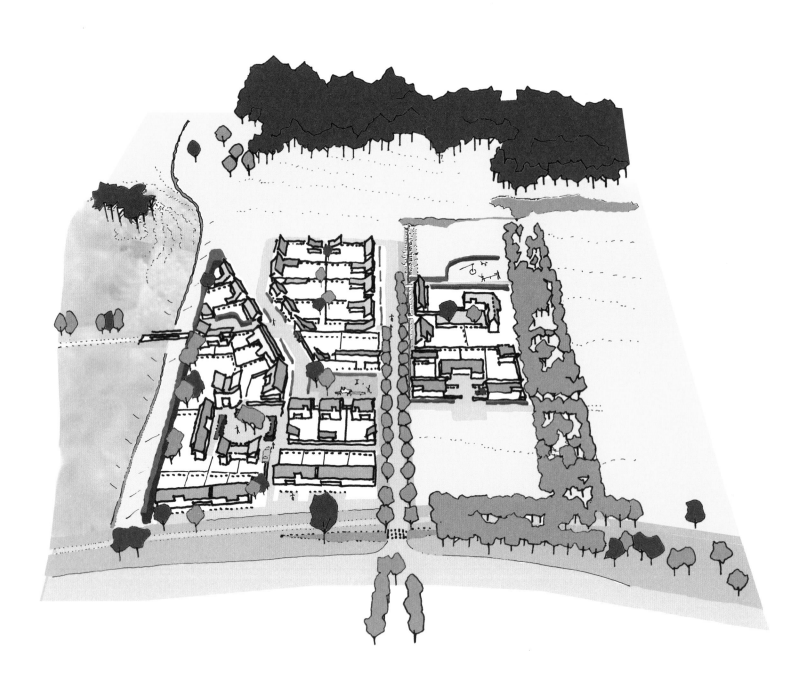

MASTERPLAN ESTABLISHMENT

The process of developing the masterplan commenced with design-orientated research into Highland settlement patterns and the local landscape. Ideas were developed and shared through a number of meetings and workshops involving the Board, the Advisory Board and statutory stakeholders [Figure 3.3]. A detailed brief and design proposal were established, which addressed particular priorities and concerns of the Board, and Advisory Board in the first instance. Examples of these included:

- Mike Greaves of The Highland Council's interest in townscape and community planning;

- Councillor Iain Ross and The Scottish Government's desires to promote of sustainable design and renewables technologies;

- Susan Torrance of Highland Housing Alliance's interest in attracting a broad range of participants by allowing commercial flexibility;

- The Expo Project Co-ordinator Fiona Porteous's interest in promoting imaginative and innovative architecture;

- The Forestry Commission Scotland and Highland Birchwood's interest in advocating timber construction and wood fuel.

The final mix and allocation of the 27 plots reflected stakeholders' intentions that, compared with the usual or typical approach whereby houses were procured by volume, in standardised kits or house types; in this case, houses were to be largely procured as individually designed prototype houses sitting in side-by-side, house-by-house comparators, with sustainable living and placemaking as key drivers.

By February 2007 the urban design of the housing layout, landscape design and technical studies had been established and endorsed. This work was reflected in the Urban Design Framework document that formed the design brief for the aforementioned RIAS competition. The design framework was published as an A3 document with a supporting Plan and an Accommodation Schedule.

" By February 2007 the urban design of the housing layout, landscape design and technical studies had been established and endorsed."

FIGURE 3 3 EXPO SITE IN CONTEXT OF WIDER LANDSCAPE

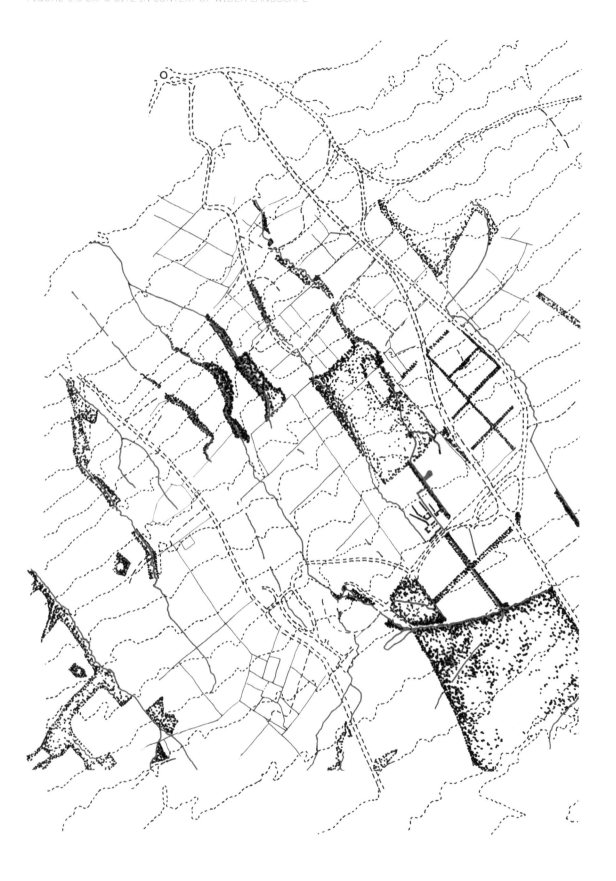

FIGURE 3.4 EXPO SITE CONTEXT PLAN

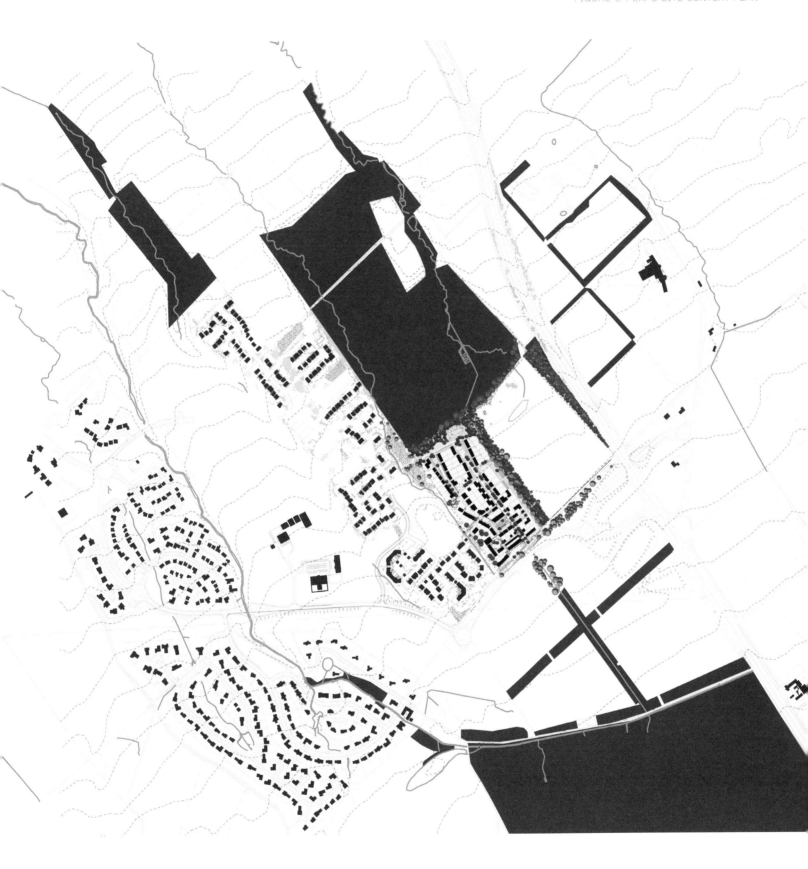

This Framework set the scene for 'place-specific' regional architecture that would contrast with the local context of volume-built and standardised private housing development. [Figure 3.4] It established a context for the architects to work with in a series of spatial scenarios. The urban design objectives included:

- the linking of frontages and elevation designs to form a coherent street environment;

- integrating front gardens and boundaries;

- the design of houses with front doors and openings to the street; and generally

- a sensitive fit into the topography and the local landscape.

The attention paid to placemaking and the use of design codes was intended to go some way towards obviating the risk of an 'architectural zoo' – in other words a random grouping of unconnected design solutions in a wide and uncontrolled palette of materials.

THE COMPETITION BRIEF

The contents of the Urban Design Framework were as follows:

Vision and Purpose

The introduction to the Framework had a clear mission – a 'rallying cry' – 'to improve the quality of architecture and design in the Highland landscape'. The vision also explained:

- the rationale for the housing mix and mix of tenure – to create a broad community;

- the design ideas for the intended street layout;

- priorities for the architecture;

- the policy context;

- and a broad vision for sustainable development encompassing energy performance standards, materials selection, themed areas within the site, and an integrated approach linking architecture and infrastructure.

Context

Section 2 contained assembled material that was intended to be informative and inspirational, including historical maps of the site and the wider landscape, site photographs, images of indigenous building and settlements, and images illustrating some of the diverse use of materials used for construction in Highland Scotland throughout time. The text promoted 'place-specific', locally adapted architecture and an imaginative use of material.

Urban Design, Public Realm and Infrastructure Design

The Framework Plan and Section 3 set down a street-by-street context for the architecture, each street and zone having variable characteristics typical of a settlement formed as an intricate response to topography and landscape. This approach gave the architects the choice of a great range of plot types, accommodation options and urban and/or rural scenarios. South Terrace, The Avenue and The Green each had very different urban characters, and quite different opportunities for architectural responses and expression such as access over a bridge, turning a street corner or designing home offices. [See Figures 3.5, 3.6 and 3.7]. There was no standard plot.

Section 3 included coded elements only where the architecture was crucial to the urban design objectives, such as frontage line and building heights. However, the code was largely abstract and non-prescriptive in terms of the architectural language and detail. There was a requirement that each house should interact with the street and community infrastructure – with the purpose of being actively designed as outward looking, or to address particular overlooking considerations in relation to neighbours. Building eaves and ridge heights were defined in sections, whilst frontage lines and footprint limitations (build areas) were defined within the framework plan. The appropriateness of applying a level of 'prescription' was much discussed at the time, however, the urban design objectives and the aim of placemaking were seen as the key essentials for the benefit of future residents.

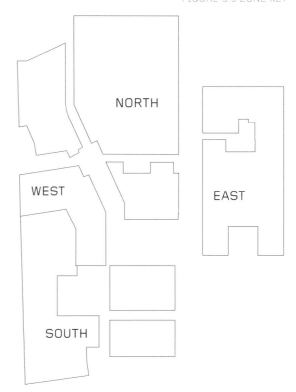

FIGURE 3.5 ZONE KEY

This gave rise to the modest level of abstract coding adopted and it proved, if anything, a more interesting context for architects to work with or play off against rather than presenting them with a blank page.

This section also set down the vision for streets designed to 'shared space' principles, prioritising pedestrians over cars. In addition, it set down the various components of community infrastructure that were to be provided, including a communal heating scheme for the whole site, (later omitted due to the exceptionally low energy requirements of the dwellings, which made the high capital cost of the scheme non-cost effective). Finally, Section 3 explained the interface of the development with the Fair as an event.

FIGURE 3.6 PLAN OF EXPO SITE

KEY

9B	Build area and house type reference
10	Plot area and reference
	Required frontage line
	Important secondary elevation
	Elevation or part elevaton without direct overlooking windows
	If building over in-curtilage parking, this should not be enclosed at street level
	Community Recycling
	Site Boundary
	Plot Boundary
	Garden Wall 1.8m high unless otherwise noted
	Deer Fence
	Rabbit-proof Fence
	Hedge 0.9m high unless otherwise noted
	Proposed Individual Trees
	Proposed Tree Belts

NOTES

1. Based on OS Superplan data. This drawing is subject to a detailed topographical survey to be established.

2. This drawing is subject to approval by the Highland Council.

3. The purpose of this drawing is to show the design intent of the urban design proposals for the Fair.

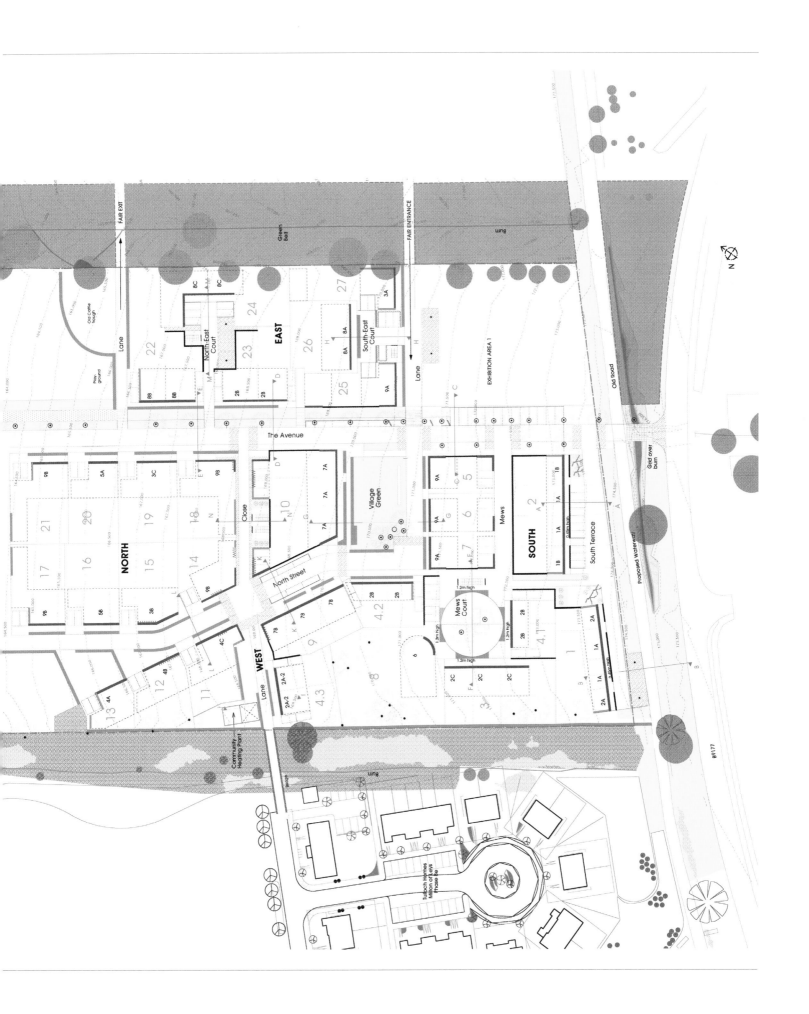

URBAN DESIGN, PUBLIC REALM AND
INFRASTRUCTURE DESIGN

Principal Street: The Avenue
This Street operates at 2 levels. On the one hand it is
the link between the B177, the Housing Fair site, and
the exhibition area to the North. On the other hand it
provides the principle transition between the poles of
man made and natural landscapes.

This street follows an avenue line derived from the
linear tree-belt to the South. It begins as hard paved
and urban. This form is then incised by channels and
stormbunds, giving way to a grassy surface water
swale and burn, deepening and widening at its end
until filled with irises and rushes. The swale is an
echo of the linear burns and drainage channels of the
wider landscape.

The street is the principal spine linking the various
other tributary streets and lanes to the main road.
It will be the most active, public and urban street
where it is close to the main road, becoming the most
secluded street at its remote end beyond the pond and
in amongst new woodland. The street will be planted
with avenue trees. These trees will, in the south zone,
frame space for visitor parking alongside the main
entrance.

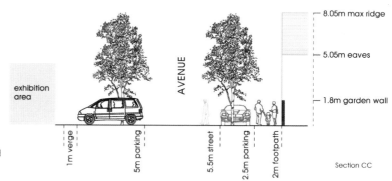

Section CC

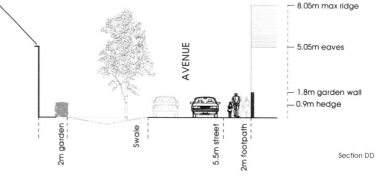

Section DD

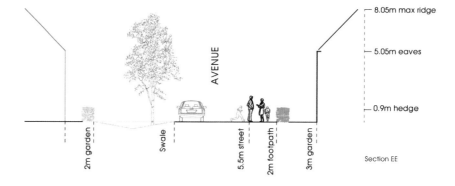

Section EE

To the west of the street a sequence of masonry garden walls is anticipated along private boundaries, linking gable-ended buildings. Like sentries these houses and ancillary buildings should provide generous windows overlooking the street and at corner points. The sequential pattern of gable ends to the west is important. There is then a set-back in the north zone to allow shallow private gardens to the detached houses beyond. Here the beech hedged garden boundaries would begin.

To the east of the street houses are reached by bridges constructed from reclaimed railway sleepers across the shallow swale. Plot 25 should have a private masonry house. This plot should provide generous windows overlooking the street. Plot 22-23 should have hedges. These houses have their long elevation and principle frontage towards the street with large windows providing good overlooking.

Paving materials will include tar-spray and gravel carriageway surfaces, Marshalls granite (or similar) paving to footways including bands of Caithness stone, and/or setts to parking areas and junctions. It is currently intended that garden boundary kerbs and paving will be in Caithness stone offcuts or using large larch sleepers. Boundary beech hedges will be backed by a temporary larch slatted fence. Street trees will be Larch and Scots Pine.

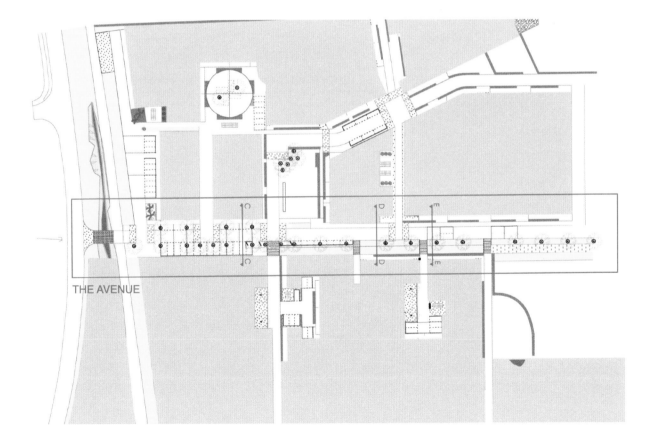

THE AVENUE

Plot Design Codes

The plot codes reflected the zone-by-zone briefing agenda of the Advisory Board. As with the street codes these avoided defining an architectural language, encouraging a diversity of ideas and innovation.

Experimentation in 'form and space, use of light, elevations, sections, technologies, construction methods and use of material' was sought in each house in the spirit of the West 8 waterfront housing at Borneo Sporenburg in Amsterdam, for example (Ref 3.1).

Simple forms and shallow plans were encouraged in response to the outcomes of research into indigenous architecture. The arrangements for on-street parking and communal refuse/re-cycling stations were explained.

Four zones within the site each had set themes and localised briefing requirements [Figure 3.8 overleaf].

Sustainability Code

This section was researched by Max Fordham and Partners who set performance standards; including a minimum standard of BRE Ecohomes 'excellent' (Ref 3.2) rating for all houses. All entrants were required to submit a Statement of Sustainable Design accompanied by a completed BRE Ecohomes proforma. Energy–efficiency targets were set [Figure 3.9] and specific technical judging criteria were also described and summarised in the competition weighting table [Figure 3.10].

	ENERGY THEME	CLADDING MATERIALS	COLOUR THEME
South Zone	Wood Fuel	ROBUST/URBAN Majority masonry / minority lightweight	Monochrome and mute – natural materials
West Zone	Solar Design	LIGHTWEIGHT/RURAL Minority masonry / majority lightweight	Colours of the landscape
North Zone	Carbon Neutrality	ROBUST/URBAN Majority masonry / minority lightweight	Monochrome and mute – natural materials
East Zone	Re-cycling	LIGHTWEIGHT/RURAL Minority masonry / majority lightweight	Colours of the landscape

FIGURE 3.9 ENERGY EFFICIENCY TARGETS

A U values

The following U values are to be complied with (generally a value 20% better than shown by the technical hand books clause 6.1.2 (2007)):

Element	U Value W/m^2.K
Walls	less than 0.20
Floors	less than 0.18
Roofs	less than 0.13
Openings	less than 1.15

B SAP 2005 Dwelling Emissions Rate (DER)

30kg CO_2 /yr.m^2 or 50% improvement over Target Emissions Rate (TER) whichever is the lower.

C Air-tightness

As the U values of a building improves air infiltration rate becomes the key component of heat loss. To address this issue the following air permeability is to be achieved: 2m^3/hr.m^2@50pa pressure

FIGURE 3.10 COMPETITION WEIGHTING TABLE

	CRITERIA	COMPETITION WEIGHTING
1	Demonstrating zone based theme	10%
2	Contribution to Highland economy and communities	20%
3	Making best use of the site, for example topography and orientation	5%
4	Enhance biodiversity and wildlife habitats	5%
5	Low-carbon design: minimise energy use through passive solar design, energy-efficient design, and use of micro-renewable	25%
6	Design to conserve water	5%
7	Design-in sustainable waste and sewage treatment facilities	5%
8	Use of sustainable materials	20%
9	Minimise waste in construction and life-time	5%

FIGURE 3.8 PLOT DESIGN CODES - FROM FRAMEWORK DOCUMENT

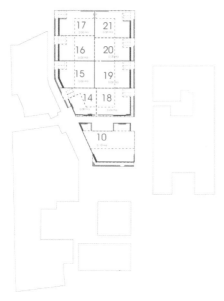

1. North zone plot key

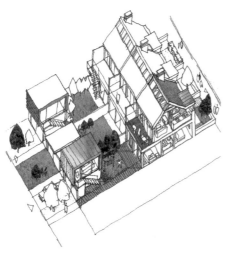

2. Proposals for dual frontage plots incorporating garages and home work units. Cottage for Millbank © Smith Scott Mullan Associates

PLOT DESIGN CODES

4.05 NORTH ZONE (PLOTS 10, 14 -21)
Local street frontage considerations

Principal building frontages must be located where show on the framework plan L-02. Plot 10 provides an important frontage interacting with the village green. Building frontages along the close behind Plot 10 are important to prevent this becoming a hidden corner of the site. Home-work units (or other active uses e.g. granny-flats or studios) should be provided over the carports on Plot 10, to overlook the lane and community, re-cycling area. Equally wrap-around house frontages and home-work units (or active uses) on Plots 14 and 18 should overlook the lane.

Plots 17 and 21 should have home/work units (or active uses) on the lane to their north to give a frontage, however these will not have a northern outlook in the long-term. Overlooking issues must be addressed in particular where shown on the framework plan.

Local street section considerations

Building scale and the design intent for frontages and gardens facing the public realm are shown on the public realm sections and on the framework plan.

Local boundary considerations

The predominant front garden boundaries in this zone are beech hedges. Masonry walls are to be installed by the plot developers adjoining the recycling areas at Plots 10, and also at Plots 14 and 18 on the other side of the close.

Local car parking considerations

Parking for all plots in-curtilage with visitor parking at the avenue.

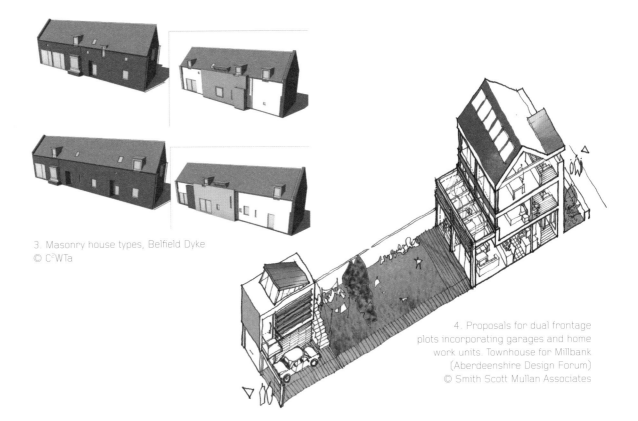

3. Masonry house types, Belfield Dyke
© C²WTa

4. Proposals for dual frontage plots incorporating garages and home work units. Townhouse for Millbank (Aberdeenshire Design Forum)
© Smith Scott Mullan Associates

Energy efficiency theme: Carbon Neutrality

The theme for energy-efficiency for this zone is Carbon-Neutrality. This should aim for zero CO_2 emissions in use. The plots in this area are large and have the capacity to use a variety of techniques for limiting carbon emissions.

Materials and colour theme

The theme for external materials in this zone is ROBUST and URBAN:

- Majority masonry wall cladding/roofing (including render)
- Minority lightweight wall cladding/roofing

The general emphasis should be on the monochrome and mute colours of natural building materials.

5. Donaghy House, Avielochan

THE COMPETITION PROCESS

The first stage of the competition was launched by the RIAS on 31 January 2007 with a submission date of 4 May 2007. 88 entries were received, all of which formed the content of an exhibition held in Inverness as part of the Six Cities Design Festival (Ref 3.3) in May-June 2007.

Technical assessment took place in early May 2007 at the RIAS by Lori McElroy (Sust. Programme and Board Member), Gary Wilson (WSD – Valuers and Quantity Surveyors) and Johnny Cadell (Cadell2 – Masterplanners for the Housing Fair).

Final judging took place in Edinburgh in mid May 2007 with Iain Ross, Mike Greaves, Max Fordham and David Page as judges, supported by Fiona Porteous and Johnny Cadell. The winners were announced on 1st June 2007.

POST – COMPETITION DESIGN DEVELOPMENT

The competition yielded an array of excellent architecture, including work from across the whole of Scotland and by some of Scotland's leading private practitioners and local authorities. Some plots proved more popular than others attracting a high level of entries, whereas for others the level of competition was less intense with fewer submissions. Overall however, the level of ambition and aspiration was remarkable.

Post-competition, the role of the framework incorporated the need to address a number of anomalies that resulted from the competition entries and the judging process.

" The competition yielded an array of excellent architecture, including work from across the whole of Scotland"

FIGURE 3.11 VIEW OF PLOTS 2 AND 5 FROM THE MAIN ENTRANCE TO THE SITE

FIGURE 3.12 VIEW FROM SOUTH WEST CORNER OF THE SITE WITH PLOT 1 IN THE FOREGROUND

For example, some plot designs and parts of the masterplan had to be significantly altered to bring all the house designs into a common framework and to include all winning entries [Figures 3.10 and 3.11]. Thus, the process had left the following issues to be addressed:

- there were no submissions for the three self-build Plots 11, 12 and 13, but as there were two excellent submissions for 3-house terraces at Plot 9 it was decided to re-locate one of these to fill the gap left by two of the self-build houses. Equally, the house designed by Trevor Black was considered suitable to fill the gap at Plot 13.

- Oliver Chapman Architects had made proposals for three plots as a single entry, Plots 22, 23 and 24 [comprising six houses in a courtyard cluster]. Given the quality of other submissions for these plots it was decided by the competition judges that Oliver Chapman Architects, Malcolm Fraser Architects and NSJR McLean should all be awarded plots and this led to a requirement for a re-design of these plots within an adjusted framework that could accommodate all three.

- The designs for Plots 14 and 15 were swapped in order that the landmark house designed by Richard Murphy was given a more prominent location.

After the competition there were several significant changes made at later stages to the masterplan design, resulting from the implementation process:

- Discussions with the planning authority had led to a requirement for a greater stand-off distance from nearby trees. This had an impact on the design of Plot 26 by Studio KAP and Plot 27 by Malcolm Fraser Architects. Plot 26 had to be partially re-designed and Plot 27 re-located.

- The wood-fuel community heating plant was removed shortly after the competition. A detailed study had shown that community heating would be uneconomical, mainly due to the estimated low heating demands of the extremely well-insulated houses, compared with high infrastructure costs for the energy centre and distribution pipes. This resulted in alterations to the design of some of the house types and left a gap, where it had been intended to site the energy plant, alongside the west gateway into the site.

- A value-engineering exercise conducted by the Highland Housing Alliance in association with its advisors and the developers led to the removal of a number of planned detached home-offices that formed part of the brief for a number of plots and which, in some cases, made important contributions to the continuity and enclosure of the intended street frontages. Value engineering also affected the materials and finishes in some of the houses. This is further explored in Chapter 6.

- The undeveloped Plot 10 (see Chapter 6 for further detail) also left a substantial gap in the planned urban structure, leaving four centrally located street frontages un-built. The vacant plot was used for the marquee, catering and the temporary Anta house (see Chapter 6) during the event. These facilities had originally been planned alongside the entrance.

- Finally, there were some elements of the infrastructure design that were not completed for the August 2010 event, due to the impact of weather-related and other delays in programme and for financial reasons. Boundary walls and street furniture were omitted. These human-scaled elements of the infrastructure were specifically designed to correlate with the architecture in terms of material and quality of detail.

Plot co-ordination

Between 2007 and 2010 as masterplanners, Cadell2 had extensive correspondence with the plot architects during implementation. Fiona Porteous – the Housing Fair Co-ordinator provided the interface for this exchange during the planning process. Infrastructure and plot drawings were lodged on an Extranet site arranged by the project manager WSD. This enabled the sharing and communication of design information between the multiple design teams involved.

Johnny Cadell, Cadell2 LLP
Masterplanner

DELIVERING THE
EXPO PROJECT

CHAPTER 4

" It was thought that in the highly
competitive Scottish housing market,
architects and developers would leap at
the chance to compete to build a house
for exhibition to the public."

FIGURE 4.1 THE EXPO SITE, MILTON OF LEYS, INVERNESS

4

In August 2005, Highland Housing Alliance (HHA) was invited to join an Advisory Board set up by The Highland Council to promote a Finnish style 'Housing Fair'. A key player in the project was the Forestry Commission Scotland, because of a desire to see increased use of Scottish Timber in Scottish construction.

The HHA is a relatively new organisation, founded in 2005 to buy land and build houses in the Highlands. It is a unique development company dedicated to building a wide variety of homes at several sites around the Highlands, it is owned by five housing associations working in the Highlands, two housing trusts and The Highland Council.

As described in previous chapters, a number of delegations had visited Finland, with The Scottish Government, to see first hand the impact of annual Housing Fairs on the aspirations of the public, and on private housing developers in terms of improving design quality. All of those who had taken part in the visits had been inspired by the concept and it was thought that in the highly competitive Scottish housing market, architects and developers would leap at the chance to show off their design and construction skills by competing to build a house for exhibition to the public. The intention was that the costs would be recouped by sale of the houses at the end of the exhibition.

THE SITE

The Highland Council and the Forestry Commission Scotland had trawled their land banks, but found nothing suitable, as many of the obvious possible sites already had planning permission for other housing projects or were inappropriate.

The Fair's Advisory Board had minimum requirements for the site, it had to:

- be easily accessible for large numbers of visitors;

- be commercially attractive to developers if they were to fund the building of the houses and to have some guarantee that they would get their money back with a successful sale;

- have guaranteed services in place, with capacity for water, sewerage and electricity;

- be reasonable to build on – no major contamination or earthworks issues;

- be zoned for housing in the Local Plan;

- and lastly, it had to be in Inverness.

A comprehensive examination of all zoned housing sites in the Inverness area resulted in a short list of four potential locations. Feasibility studies were carried out on all four options, none of which proved suitable. There was also the hurdle of the fact that any landowner in 2006 with a fully serviced zoned site would be looking for upwards of £400,000 an acre. Two developers, Robertson Homes and Tullochs were approached, but the housing boom at that time meant that they were both reluctant to part with sites at a reasonable price.

A site was finally identified at Balvonie, adjacent to the Milton of Leys Masterplan area. The site was owned by Tulloch, but was not zoned for housing in the current local plan. The Reporter in 2005 had specifically mentioned it as possible for future zoning, given that it was a natural extension to the existing Milton of Leys housing developments. The site was landlocked, and Tulloch also owned the area of land that linked it to the adopted road. They had also invested substantially in bringing all services adjacent to the site. It fitted every criteria with the exception of the zoning, but was further out of Inverness than had been the original intention.

In 2006, Milton of Leys had around 450 houses, but no community facilities. A site had been zoned for a neighbourhood shopping centre and school, but neither had yet materialised. The area was also cut off from the other South Western suburbs of Wester Inshes and Raigmore by the lack of a link road, forcing traffic to go on to the main A9 trunk road to go anywhere from Milton of Leys.

The addition of the Housing Fair development could potentially increase the number of houses at Milton of Leys to a level that would necessitate the completion of the Link Road. The HHA therefore agreed to contribute to the Link Road as part of the development costs of the Fair. However, the purchase was contingent on obtaining an outline planning consent and confirmation that the site was able to be developed.

The outline planning application was made for the development of the site, and while all notice periods were observed, and meetings held with the local Community Councils, the idea of the Fair became tangled in existing community concerns about the lack of facilities at Milton of Leys. Further, because the site had not yet been designed, the community expressed concern about what it would actually look like, and at that point no one was in a position to respond with the details. While outline consent was granted, it came with a full list of detailed conditions, the major one of which was the formation of a masterplan for the site.

FIGURE 4.2 EXPO SITE, JUNE 2008

THE COMPETITION

Two appointments were made at this time – a Project Co-ordinator, Fiona Porteous, an architect, and, after a tender process, the masterplanner Johnny Cadell of Cadell2 and his team. However, before anything else could move on, decisions had to be made about how to develop the site, what financial model would be used, and also how best to run the competition. The first decision was to appoint the Royal Incorporation of Architects in Scotland (RIAS) to organise the competition on the basis of a masterplan developed by Cadell2 around an agreed mix of houses, tenures and sizes: 23 affordable, rented and low cost home ownership and 32 private houses for sale.

There were plots assigned to flats, terraces and semi-detached dwellings as well as large detached houses resulting in a design competition for 27 plots. A detailed site plan and design brief were drawn up, showing building lines, eaves heights, an indication of preferred materials, technologies, orientation and relationships between buildings: all of which were dependent on site location. Some plots specified live-work units, either within the house or within the plot curtilage. Financial information was also provided, particularly in relation to the affordable units, which had to meet the budgets set by The Scottish Government.

The funding model invited architects to team up with a developer to submit an entry, and the winning teams would then work up the designs and buy the land from the HHA as a fully serviced plot on which to build their houses. HHA would use the plot price to refund the purchase price of the land, the infrastructure contract and the masterplan and planning fees. The amount of land acquired was sufficient to enable a Phase 2 development after the event.

The competition was run in early 2007 and resulted in 88 entries from which the winners were selected in May 2007. At this stage in was envisaged that the event would run in August 2009 and a two-year build period seemed reasonable.

FIGURE 4.3 EXPO SITE, NOVEMBER 2009

FIGURE 4.4 EXPO SITE, FEBRUARY 2010

It became apparent over 2007 that some architects had not yet identified a developer and that some designs while architecturally iconic, would struggle to meet cost constraints. The most dramatic example was the NORD Plot 2 terrace of 4, clad in Caithness Stone and submitted as an affordable design, another being the house selected for Plot 10. This was designated as an 'affordable' plot for rental via a housing association, but the selected design was originally designed as a private house for sale. And there were other similar issues relating to houses that had been designed for one plot having been selected as winners but on a different plot.

Given that there was no up front finance, the HHA in some instances had to front-fund the cost of working up detailed planning and building warrant drawings for some practices. There was also the issue of conflicts between developers and architects on the value engineering issues and the viability of some designs (this is further discussed in Chapter 8). Convincing major developers not used to working in the Highlands about the realities of local price values and revenues was also challenging.

At the end of 2007, the HHA commissioned site preparation and infrastructure works, from its own resources. The infrastructure contractor was awarded a series of small contracts which enabled the pace of works to be varied dependent on progress elsewhere.

By 2008, detailed planning consent had been obtained for all the houses and for the masterplan and the majority of building warrants were programmed for submission.

The HHA was attempting to complete plot purchases, but by now, the effects of the banking crisis were beginning to affect the programme. Developers were beginning to withdraw from the project and unless a new finance model could be found, was put in place, the project was in danger of collapsing.

In the meantime, Councillor Jean Urquhart had replaced Councillor Iain Ross as Chairman of the Advisory Board, which was transformed into a legal company. The Board decided that, given the extended timescale, there was an opportunity to raise the profile of the event nationally. They decided on a change of name and so the Fair was rebranded – Scotland's Housing Expo – at which point it was also agreed that the event would be postponed until August 2010.

Alex Neil, MSP, the Minister for Housing and Communities, was approached, to explore funding options. The proposal was that the 23 houses for rent/low cost home ownership would be financed by Housing Association Grant (HAG). Given the problem of securing developers due to the financial crisis, the build contracts for all the houses were split between 5 major house builders who already operated in the Highlands and who each already had declared an interest in a plot – Tulloch Homes Express, Robertson Highland, O'Brien Properties, Morrison Homes and William Gray Construction – in return for them proceeding to finance their original plots. Plot 17 had been funded up-front. This left 24 houses to be financed. The HHA took out a bank loan which was underwritten by a guarantee from The Scottish Government.

" At the end of 2007, the HHA commissioned site preparation and infrastructure works, from its own resources."

FIGURE 4.5 EXPO SITE, APRIL 2010

The decision was also made to proceed on a design and build basis, which was controversial with the architects and some members of the Expo Board, but which was deemed necessary for cost control. WSD were appointed as cost consultants and had to negotiate with each architect and developer to deliver each plot within a target budget — which in most cases still exceeded the then projected revenue from the house sales. The architects had to absorb the fact that there was no additional grant support available for innovation and no value attributed in mortgage valuations for whole life cost savings or carbon footprint reduction — despite these being driving forces for the competition.

Although there was backing from The Scottish Government, no finance was made available by the bank until April 2010. In the meantime, the HHA had agreed to pay 70% of the fees for the 24 houses it was funding. Given the enormous financial pressures most practices were under at this time, compounded by the excessively hard winter of 2009, there was no option but to front fund these.

The contractors in some instances were able to get on site in December 2009, but the main build work did not really commence until February 2010 for an opening in August 2010.

Good site organisation was imperative, and new legal structures — the Highland Contractors Consortium — were put in place to cover insurance issues and common compounds and cabin areas worked well. There was also a special arrangement made to allow a sixth contractor on site — James MacQueen from the Isle of Skye on Plot 17 with Rural Design Architects, who had shown extreme faith in the project from the outset having been the only developer who paid up-front for this Plot in 2008.

The infrastructure contractor, GF Job was still on site to complete the masterplanned street scape alongside the other builders. And, the landscaping company, Tillhill, had to complete gardens while the weather continued to make life difficult for everyone.

Snow, ice, floods and fire were added difficulties on site from January 2010 onwards. However, slowly but surely some amazing buildings started to appear from the ground as progress was being made.

The event also lost Fiona Porteous in May 2010, but found a replacement in Fiona Hampton to help bring the event to fruition by August. The amount of organisation involved was significant, and several omissions had to be overcome, such as no budget for floor coverings or the children's play area – which was finally realised through the expertise of Wayne and Geraldine Hemmingway, who had supported the project from the outset in 2007.

July was a hectic month. Meeting after meeting saw items ironed out and resolved, with the added spice of the event organisers arriving to sort out the logistics of staging a month long event. Meanwhile the contractors pulled out every stop to ensure all requirements for the event were met – toilets, café, ramps, etc.

The Saturday before the opening and the Sunday morning of the first of August were a sight to behold, with people running everywhere. There was a skip in the middle of the main street, which was so full, it could hardly be moved – but it was finally removed – and the site was as tidy as we could make it in the pouring rain. From 10am onwards, people began to arrive and kept on coming and were in the main, amazed.

We had dealt with scepticism from the local press from the outset in 2006, and despite reports of a slow start the reputation and achievement of Scotland's (first) Housing Expo was gaining ground, and the tide eventually turned in its favour. The completion of the Link Road and the building of the new Milton of Leys primary school helped change local opinion and while the traffic generated by the 33,000 people who visited the event was at times an issue, in the main it has been welcomed.

THE RESULT

50 out of the original 55 houses were completed on time. Plot 10, a terrace of 3, was not built in the end because of cost issues (see Chapter 6). Plots 16 and 21 were to be constructed of massive timber imported from Austria, and were not built in time for the event, although Plot 16 had its frame erected, and so the only empty Plot was 21, which has since been completed.

Finally, at the start of 2011, people are beginning to move into the houses, turning Scotland's first Housing Expo into the Braes of Balvonie – a community in what Wayne Hemmingway has described as the best housing development in the UK.

FIGURE 4.6 EXPO SITE, JUNE 2010

The HHA has 24 private houses to sell in order to repay the bank and release The Scottish Government guarantee – no small feat in the financial climate of 2011, but huge lessons have been learned:

- we need to find ways to fund innovation and to encourage use of local materials which may be more expensive, but local manufacturers also need to undertake product development to compete with continental imports;

- the same message is true for the promotion and use of Scottish timber, a cause which in some ways prompted the Expo, but which needs concentrated research and development work;

- the financial equation does not add up at the moment and developers are being asked to fund higher than current building regulation requirements with no added value for a post 2010 Building Standard Regulations house.

However, we have established what it means to deliver an Expo and the level of interest amongst the general public exceeded expectation. Undoubtedly, an Expo in a more central location should attract significantly higher visitor numbers – one difference between Scotland and Finland that should be considered is that in Finland, municipalities compete and donate the site, which was a significant cost factor in our case.

Susan Torrance
Chief Executive HHA

_____

" We have established what it means to deliver an Expo and the level of interest amongst the general public exceeded expectation."

_____

THE EXPO EVENT

" The intention of the event was to
provide a 'test bed' for design,
construction and technological
innovation. It was hoped that by
exposing the public to new ideas,
developers would be inspired to learn
new skills and source fresh ideas to
incorporate into future designs."

FIGURE 5.1

CHAPTER 5

BEYOND THE HOUSES

The whole process of creating this ambitious project for the first time in the UK involved a significant learning curve for everyone, including the architects. The result was the creation of 52 diverse, unique and visionary interpretations of future living, all set in an overall vision for community living created by Cadell2.

However, the completion of the houses was only the first stage in the process. The next challenge was to open the houses as a public event with the results on display for a month, throughout August 2010. Compared with selling a development from the traditional showhome concept, whereby developers have one house completed in advance, in the case of the Expo, the site had to be completed to a standard that complied with the health and safety and accessibility requirements that would be applied to any public event. There was also a dedicated event management team employed by The Highland Council, which included supervisory staff and 'house ambassadors' (mainly construction-related students) who were trained to be able to describe the features of the specific houses they were assigned to any visitor who cared to ask. This type of bespoke service is not offered in the Finnish model, where the invigilation of houses is left to the developer or the architect responsible for delivery.

During the month-long Scottish Housing Expo the houses and their contents provided a platform for showcasing a wealth of Scottish design talent, including interior and product design. The intention of the event was to provide a 'test bed' for design, construction and technological innovation, with a view to informing Scottish house building in the future and to test these ideas on the public. It was hoped that by exposing the public to new ideas, developers would be inspired to learn new skills and source fresh ideas to incorporate into future designs. At the same time, the Expo demonstrated how new building standards could be met in terms of energy efficiency and carbon reduction.

SPONSORS

In Finland, in addition to providing the opportunity to explore the houses, a great deal of effort goes into securing sponsorship in the form of furnishings and fittings for interiors, street furniture, gardens and landscaping. This is backed up by a substantial exhibition and 'trade village', giving visitors a chance not only to see fully decorated show-homes, but also the opportunity to see wider ranges of merchandise from the suppliers responsible for the interiors, gardens, etc.

This being the first event of its kind in Scotland, there was no precedent that could be drawn upon to entice potential sponsors of the benefit of getting involved, and this element of the event had to rely on the dogged determination of the Project Co-ordinator, Fiona Porteous and latterly her successor Fiona Hampton. The difficulty in convincing sponsors to take a chance on the Expo was compounded by slow progress on site during the extremely long and cold winter of 2009/10 and a few who had expressed an interest dropped out as the weather worsened – not confident that the event would come to fruition. However, some local companies recognised the opportunities and some major international companies that had been involved in such things before remained confident. In the end, sponsorship of one kind or another was forthcoming from over 70 organisations (not including the contractors and architects who had put in considerable in-kind effort), and those who participated appeared to find their involvement worthwhile.

THE EVENT

The event opened on time at 10am on the 1st August and despite the pouring rain, there was a queue of people at the ticket office as the last debris was removed from site to comply with the Council's event safety requirements.

For the whole of August, visitors were able to view 50 completed houses – 20 of which were partially or fully furnished and 12 of which housed exhibitions or events. 18 were unfurnished including 6 flats and some terraced houses that were identical to furnished neighbouring units.

For real enthusiasts or those without the luxury of time on their hands, the whole site could be viewed in a single day, but the option of an upgrade from a single day ticket to a multi-pass return ticket was taken up by 2,500 of the 30,000 plus people who visited the event. An on-site café provided by Cobbs, a local Inverness-shire based company, provided respite for day trippers and a chance to catch up with old friends for return visitors. Perhaps due to the excellent fare on offer or the success of the event in attracting visitors, the café was often overcrowded especially on very good days and in bad weather – a key lesson for the future.

" Sponsorship was forthcoming from over 70 organisations (not including the in-kind effort of the contractors and architects), and those who participated appeared to find their involvement worthwhile."

FIGURE 5.2

FIGURE 5.3 PLOT 17

FIGURE 5.4 PLOT 22

FIGURE 5.5 PLOT 9

FIGURE 5.6 PLOT 15

FIGURE 5.7 PLOT 7

FIGURE 5.8 PLOT 11

FIGURE 5.9 PLOT 18

FIGURE 5.10 PLOT 4.1

FIGURE 5.11 CLAYSTATION: REMODELLING HOME

SITE SIGNAGE

Site signage is an important feature of the Finnish Fairs in terms of providing information on the features of the house; from room numbers to energy performance to sponsors. Here we adopted similar approach and each house had an information board with a house description provided by the architect, displaying key features from room numbers to materials used and energy performance predictions based on Building Warrant applications.

In order to entertain children, this information was summarised on small trump-type cards that could be collected for each house. This also provided adults interested in buying or renting a particular house with something to remind them of the plot number and other details. Unfortunately, house prices were not available in this instance prior to going to print.

Information boards explaining other site and masterplan features were dotted around the site. The signage designed by local Inverness company Dynam, was not only colourful and informative, but provided a theme that tied the whole site together (see Figure 5.20).

EXHIBITIONS

Exhibition opportunities were taken up by a variety of organisations and were available for audiences of all ages. These ranged from entertainment and young children's activities such as 'giant' chess, face painting, stilt walking, through educational activities for young and older visitors – including seminars, workshops and exhibitions. All of these challenged visitors to think beyond the Expo Event to possibilities for the future in a sustainable Scotland.

Major highlights included:

Claystation: Remodelling Home

Claystation (Ref 5.1), run by Architecture + Design Scotland, which provided an opportunity for visitors to model their own Expo House in modelling clay and then to and locate it wherever they wanted to on a giant map of the Expo. The more technically minded could locate it elsewhere in the World, via a Google Map site. Remodelling Home offered an opportunity for visitors to Scotland's Housing Expo to take creative control and collectively reshape Scotland's homes, streets, towns and cities, to propose a new participatory design model of housing for Scotland in the 21st century. This participatory exhibition provided encouragement to those who live and work in Scotland and beyond, not to merely take a closer look at the houses and spaces around them, but to be active in their rethinking and designing the built environment around them.

FIGURE 5.12 EXHIBITION STANDS

New Start Highland

New Start Highland (Ref 5.2) helps people maintain their homes through a furniture supply, housing support and a decorating service. They also provide a range of training opportunities for people finding it difficult to secure employment. At the Expo, New Start Highland furnished four of the Cairn Housing Association properties on Plot 1 using recycled and donated furniture, demonstrating not only how stylish reused furniture can be, but also what a great range of furniture New Start can supply.

Edinburgh International Science Festival

The Edinburgh Science festival (Ref 5.3) hosted the Cosy Cosy Game Show on a daily basis throughout the event. This activity consists of a game show for parents and children in which they are challenged to work out how to stop heat leaking from model houses. The game is played against the clock against other participating teams with the objective of trying to beat those around you by saving the most energy – and money!

The Highland Council Countryside Rangers

The Highland Council Countryside Rangers (Ref 5.4) provided a daily programme during the Expo of family activities from mini beast-hunts to wildlife gardening to show that even new housing developments are home to a variety of wildlife. These activities varied from day to day, ranging from making a mini-beast home or bat box, to planting some wildflower seeds or creating a frog friendly log pile, subject to visitor demand and the weather.

Sust. House

This exhibition showcased the work of Sust.: Architecture + Design Scotland's Sustainability in Architecture Programme (Ref 5.5) which had provided support to the Expo from the outset. Sust. explores the barriers and opportunities to delivering sustainable design. It acts as a catalyst for mainstreaming 'green' thinking in the built environment by providing support to live projects in partnership with a wide range of organisations, including communities, construction professionals, academic institutions, young people and client groups. For more information see – www.sust. org – a web resource giving access to a wide variety of sustainability information, resources and guidance suitable for a broad audience.

Spaces of Labour

Spaces of Labour (Ref 5.6) explores the relationship between architecture, design and Scotland's economic future. The exhibition investigated the view that the long-term future of the Scottish economy is dependent on the expansion and re-invigoration of the manufacturing and industrial sector. Architecture has a key role to play by imagining what innovative types of productive landscape might emerge in areas such as energy production, eco-transport systems, and green building materials. At the same time, the exhibition looked at how we value the historical places and buildings associated with our declining industries: coal, textiles, fishing and slate. It also speculated whether it is possible to regenerate these by finding new uses for these buildings and infrastructure.

FIGURE 5.13 SUST. HOUSE EXHIBITION

5.14 SPACES OF LABOUR EXHIBITION

FIGURE 5.15

FIGURE 5.16

FIGURE 5.17

ANTA HOUSE

ANTA (Ref 5.7), a partnership between designers Annie & Lachan Stewart and the craftsmen and women with whom they work provided one of the few retail opportunities on site. ANTA is an interior design and architecture company, specialising in home grown products. The team set up a shop in an 'ANTA House' on the vacant plot 10 and attracted a lot of interest in their SAVE (Sustainable, Affordable, Vernacular, Ecological) house and natural products and fabrics.

TIMBERPLAY PLAY AREA

For almost a decade, Timberplay have pioneered natural play design, by incorporating natural play equipment and exceptional design into everyday play spaces from schools and nurseries, public parks, leisure sites, visitor attractions and even city centres. With the support of Wayne and Geraldine Hemingway, who championed the event from the outset, the Housing Expo was lucky enough to secure a play area designed by Timberplay, which catered for, and was a real hit with children of all ages, providing an innovative, exciting and completely new play experience.

Other exhibitors included – Aggregates Industries, Invisible Heating Systems, MAKAR Ltd/Neil Sutherland Architects, National House-Building Council (NHBC), Registers of Scotland, RoWAN – Waste Action and Composting and Recycling, Scots Pine Resource, Russwood, the Scottish Ecological Design Association and the Scottish Passive House Centre.

SEMINARS

There was a range of seminars and activities in and around the Expo to attract all ages, many with an eco-friendly and sustainable living theme. They aimed to educate and inform visitors about the ethos of the Expo and the concepts and building methods used for each property. Two notable examples were:

Sust. Seminars

A series of professionally orientated seminars organised by Architecture + Design Scotland's Sust. Programme, which offered an opportunity for housing and building specialists to hear and debate with expert opinion on a range of special interest topics related to the industry. These seminars were organised around linked themes each week in order that those delegates who wished to have time to explore the Expo fully would have a reason to stay in Inverness for more than one day.

Themes included:

Week 1: Contextual Planning and Architectural Responses,

Week 2: Design Frameworks and Lessons from Europe,

Week 3: Sustainability, Materials and Energy Supply,

Week 4: Ecological Design – Where next? and The Future for Scottish Timber in Construction.

The seminars were run in association with various organisations including the Royal Incorporation of Architects in Scotland, Inverness Architectural Association, Homes for Scotland, the Scottish Ecological Design Association, the Forestry Commission Scotland, and the Centre for Timber Engineering (Edinburgh Napier University). They included contributions from the Expo masterplanner, the house designers and developers, local architects, The Scottish Government, and the University of Strathclyde and local authority planners, with further contributions from other European experts and the people behind delivering an Expo in Scotland.

Housing Policy Reform Debate

The Architecture and Place Division of The Scottish Government's Directorate for the Built Environment organised two events at the Expo around The Scottish Government's engagement with the public on housing policy reform and the web-based 'Fresh thinking, New ideas' discussion (Ref 5.8). The particular theme that these two events explored was 'Quality and Place'.

Other Seminars included the topics: Passive House, Registers of Scotland, Scottish Timber in Construction, Sustainable Urban Drainage and a number of the site exhibitors ran product-specific events.

FIGURE 5.18 MY SUST. HOUSE GAMES

POINTS FOR THE FUTURE

All in all, as an event the first Scottish Housing Expo had something for everyone. There was no guideline to work from and in many ways the process of delivering the event had to be created from scratch, while drawing on the experience of partners and dialogue with the Finnish Housing Fair Co-operative in specific areas of expertise. The visits to Finland had acted as an initial inspiration, but some new key elements were added in response to The Scottish Government's and The Highland Council's own priorities. An example of the differences between this event and the projects studied in mainland Europe is the use of local materials, which seems to come naturally in other countries, but which proved a real challenge to deliver in Scotland. However, there were no standard plots and no standard solutions, unlike the Finnish model, where at least some regular solutions had been adopted over the last 40 years. When the Expo project was initiated in 2005, it had been agreed that high ambitions should be set in order to maximise what could be achieved. In the end the outcome far exceeded many people's expectations.

There were elements that were not delivered at all. And notwithstanding the architectural and landscape elements of this (which are discussed in Chapters 6 and 8), how to manage delivery of the items discussed below should be considered for any future such event.

One over-riding ambition that was not fulfilled was the intention to have a 'trade village' of exhibition and retail areas. Two impacts of this were a missed opportunity to use this to grow sponsorship and the number of houses that

FIGURE 5.19 ANTA HOUSE

remained unfurnished or partly furnished. In addition, feedback from visitors indicated disappointment in the lack of opportunities to spend money and to engage with suppliers – from construction companies and energy system suppliers to soft furnishing designers and retailers.

But the sponsors listed in the Reference section at the end of the book did take up exhibition space in the marquee, independently on-site or in unfurnished areas of some of the houses.

Lessons for the future are discussed further in Chapter 7 in relation to the Event and Chapter 8 with regard to the delivery of the houses from the viewpoint of some of the architects. At the time of writing, The Scottish Government is undertaking a review of all aspects of the Expo, this will explore in greater detail some of the issues raised here anecdotally.

Lori McElroy
Kate Hendry
Graeme McKirdy

FIGURE 5.20 EXPO COLLECTABLE TRUMP-STYLE CARDS

THE EXPO AS BUILT

CHAPTER

6

" The urban design of the Streets of the
Expo [collectively the buildings and the
spaces in-between] is a considered
response to the local landscape and to
contemporary living in the Highlands.
It seeks a sense of place and a sense
of community."

FIGURE 6.1

FIGURE 6.2

KEY

→ Bridge

— Waterway

— Building Line

FIGURE 6.5

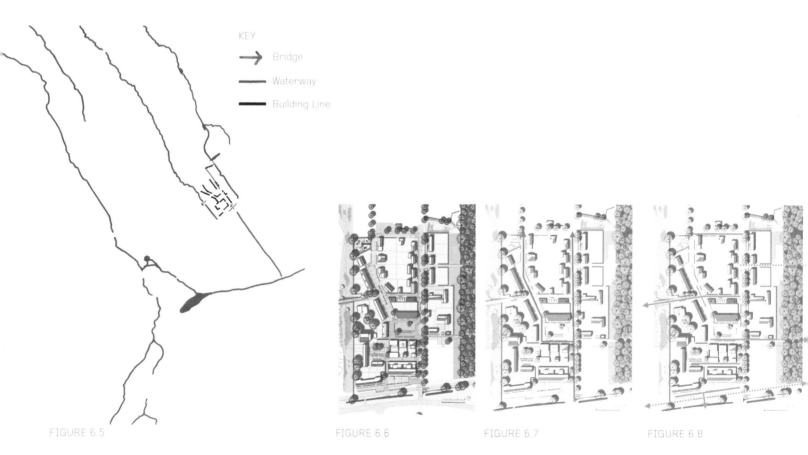

FIGURE 6.6   FIGURE 6.7   FIGURE 6.8

CHAPTER 6

THE STREETS AND SPACES OF THE EXPO

The urban design of the Streets of the Expo [collectively the buildings and the spaces in-between] is a considered response to the local landscape and to contemporary living in the Highlands. It seeks to create a sense of place and a sense of community, designed by collaboration between the masterplanners and the plot architects. [Figures 6.1 and 6.2] and [Figures 6.3 and 6.4]

PLACE AND LANDSCAPE

The upland landscape surrounding the site at Balvonie was the inspiration for the masterplan layout of the Expo. [Figure 6.5] The new streets are intertwined with tree-lines, water channels, bridges and causeways, creating a strong link to the surrounding landscape. With Drumossie Moor to the south and the forest of Balvonie Wood with its burns and gorges to the north, the 18th century parkland and tree belts surrounding the site become integrated as part of a distinctive and historically rich landscape.

The layout is planned to be highly legible and user-friendly [Figure 6.6], with a clear hierarchy in contrast with the nearby volume housing at Milton of Leys where the road infrastructure dominates. A bridge at the entrance leads to a tree-lined avenue going down the eastern side of the site towards woodland, adopting the line of an 18th century tree belt further south. In turn, a sloping brae provides the main access route down the western side leading to the play space and with an expansive view to the distant landscape of the Moray Firth. The Brae and Avenue meet at the central Green, a pedestrianised area and the central public space for the community [Figure 6.7]. The next level in the hierarchy is designed to provide routes and service spaces in lanes, paths and closes comparable with medieval patterns of settlement. These take the form of a parallel [topographically influenced] series of informal walking routes [Figure 6.8] and a location for home offices, community recycling, parking space and mews houses. The same routes link to the countryside and to local services in Milton of Leys, providing an open and permeable network without cul-de-sacs.

FIGURE 6.3

FIGURE 6.4

CONTEMPORARY LIVING

The streets and housing layout are inspired by the sociable qualities of settlements in the Highlands such as crofting communities with their nearby common grazing areas where farming work was shared in winter time, or Hirta, St Kilda where an island parliament was held outdoors on the street [Figure 6.9].

A series of innovative urban design strategies have been used at the Expo, geared towards a more sociable, healthy and sustainable lifestyle; and a safer, sheltered and inspiring residential environment.

Roads Design Innovations – Shared streets

Using principles similar to those in Hans Monderman's Woonerf (Ref 6.1) the Expo is an example of the Shared Space design philosophy, taking forward earlier work by Cadell2 at Craigmillar (Ref 6.2) in particular These principles have had a profound influence on the design of the streets and – through the design code – on the architecture. The shared space concept aims for a reconciliation of life on residential streets with cars and other vehicles, establishing safe walking and cycling routes and balancing the experience of all users in favour of pedestrians and children playing, thus encouraging a more active and lively use of streets. It also leads to a street character that is quite different from the current Scottish residential suburb – with joined-up buildings and joined-up routes – the antithesis of the cul-de-sac.

FIGURE 6.9

The experience changes drivers' perceptions using narrow streets, sharp corners, street trees, on-street parking and a strong pattern of paving highlighting pedestrian use. Through the Design Code developed for the Expo there is a strong sense of street enclosure – front gardens have been kept shallow at 0-3m – frontages at minimum of 1.5 storeys.

" A series of innovative urban design strategies have been used at the Expo; geared towards a more sociable, healthy and sustainable lifestyle, and a safer, sheltered and inspiring residential environment"

Sustainable Materials

Ground modelling, paving texture and a strong palette of natural, locally sourced and re-cycled materials are used to create a distinct character for each of the series of street types [Figures 6.10 and 6.11]. One example is the recycled setts from central Inverness that were used to create a strong tactile texture at street corners. Another is the bridges over the surface-water swale that runs alongside the Avenue, constructed from recycled hardwood rail sleepers. The design of the bridges and other street furniture were inspired by the vernacular use of timber sleepers in the Spey valley for bridges, fences and small buildings.

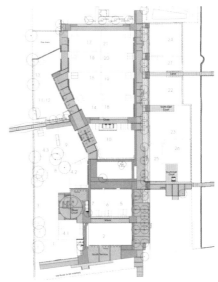

FIGURE 6.11

FIGURE 6.10

FIGURE 6.12 THE DRUM BO'NESS

FIGURE 6.13 THE DRUM BO'NESS

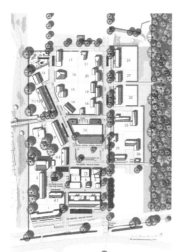

FIGURE 6.14

FIGURE 6.15

" The design of the central Green and the Play Space characterises a general approach of making outdoor public spaces that are enjoyable and well used"

Public Space

The design of the central Green and the play space characterises a general approach of making outdoor public spaces that are enjoyable and well-used [Figure 6.12 and 6.13]. When completed, the Green will be an enclosed and sheltered public space. Three houses on Plot 10 at the south edge will complete the space but were un-built in August 2010. The Green is at the meeting place of walking and cycling routes forming a focal picnic and barbecue area for the local community. The well equipped play space is designed to allow for children from 2 to 12 years to play together safely. These spaces form part of the network of routes, pocket parks, streets corners and meeting places across the site that provide safe and supportive environments for outdoor activities, children's play and a physically active lifestyle.

Community Elements

A number of other elements of the infrastructure seek to foster a sense of place and community including 50% of parking on street [Figure 6.14] and community re-cycling stations in place of individual private bins [Figure 6.15]. The innovative mix also includes home offices at street level in certain key locations to facilitate local small businesses ventures or simply working from home to limit commuting to the office. The Mews leading to Balvonie Square is a particular example with houses on both sides having detached office or studio units with separate entrances fronting onto a shared Close.

Johnny Cadell, Cadell2 LLP
Kate Hendry
Graeme McKirdy
The Architects

" A number of other elements of the infrastructure seek to foster a sense of place and community including 50% of parking on-street and community re-cycling stations in place of individual private bins"

---

1 STEALTH TERRACE

The Plot 1 terrace appealed to us as a practice as it is a typology that addresses frontage and is both at home in the city and the countryside. We were intrigued by the linear strength of groups of farmworker's cottages, long low byres and sheds but also by the idea of a new vernacular language that is both familiar and contemporary.

How does an architect design housing in the landscape and how can the interiors, even in simple dwellings, relate to a sense of space within? Our three aims in this regard were to explore the issues of form, materiality and space. On form, one of our aims was to explore the language of hips, gables and dormers which in many instances is often undervalued or utilised to 'dress up' standard developer house types. We feel that the role of these traditional elements from a formal, material and spatial perspective is worth exploration.

KEY DESIGN FEATURES
A strong feature of many rural house types is that they are traditionally 1½ storeys and the roof volume becomes part of the occupied living space. This can lead to a massing which has an affinity with traditional low-eaved housing.

With that in mind our project for the Stealth Terrace has an asymmetrical cross section with a 1 and ½ storey front and a slightly higher rear façade to ensure the floor area required to the upper floor bedrooms is achieved. The overall effect is to give a low eaves height to the front and a more sculpted gable form. The roof has been designed to give identity to both gables, one adjacent to the neighbouring Nord Terrace and the other addressing a neighbouring housing development. The new terrace comprises of four 2-3 bedroom houses with flexible living spaces on the upper floors.

Each of the houses has a double height volumes link in the living room and hall spaces. These to other living study/spaces where families can have degrees of privacy or the option to interact with each other. All living volumes are south facing to maximise daylight and solar gain potential.

With its black rubber cladding and ivy clad walls, 'Stealth Terrace', aims to have a subtle presence in the landscape.

CONSTRUCTION SYSTEM
The terrace is wrapped in a black edpm (elastic damp-proof membrane) cladding to the south, east and west façades. The north is clad in black stained larch cladding. Climbing ivy is planted along the south, east and west elevations which will grow and envelope the building transforming it into a living structure.

The building is constructed in locally produced JJI joist timber frame: a wall and roof construction that offers the opportunity to create interior volumes in the roof space. This construction system allowed for the superstructure and envelope to be completed in 4 weeks.

LESSONS LEARNED/KEY MESSAGES
- An exploration of tradition in a contemporary manner
- The importance of the roof form in rural housing
- Internal spatial innovation in living spaces
- Cost effective, sustainable yet contemporary materials
- Fast construction
- Low running costs
- A home with identity.

FIRST FLOOR

GROUND FLOOR

HOUSE NAME	Stealth Terrace
ARCHITECT	JM Architects
CONTRACTOR	Morrison Homes
OWNER/ DEVELOPER	Cairn Housing Association
HOUSE TYPE	Terrace of 4 houses
INTERNAL FLOOR AREA	end terrace - 103m²
	mid terrace - 104m²
NUMBER OF BEDROOMS	end terrace - 2
	mid terrace - 3
NUMBER OF PUBLIC ROOMS	end terrace - 2
	mid terrace - 1
PREDICTED ANNUAL HEATING COST	£92
SAP RATING	
ENERGY USAGE (HEATING ONLY) IN kWh/m²	114 kWh/m²

FIGURE 1

FIGURE 2

FIGURE 3

FIGURE 4

FIGURE 5

FIGURE 6

2

THE STONE HOUSE

The 'Stone House' is a terrace of four family sized houses, each orientated around a private garden with the upper levels having access to a private terrace. As the name suggests, the building is externally constructed from Caithness stone.

Early design directions explored the building mass in relation to the public/private aspects of the home, both to the front and rear of the house plot. At the front, the door threshold is extended to a front 'shared' garden to encourage neighbours and the passer-by to interact with the occupant of the house. At the rear of the plot, connected through the kitchen space, the principle of an 'out building' is reinterpreted as a habitable wall, with functional facilities connected back into the home: pantry, utility, storage, greenhouse, refuse, drying area, office or workshop. The plans have been developed to offer flexibility within the accommodation with the potential for an open plan living area on the upper level and the cellular bedroom spaces on the ground floor level or if preferred, a more traditional plan with the living area on the ground floor and bedrooms above.

KEY DESIGN FEATURES

Stone traditionally can create two distinct impressions in buildings. In large buildings it stands for wealth, power, and permanence, but, especially when used at a domestic scale and based on local craft traditions, it appears modest and natural. The heaviness of the stone (the Caithness stone wall to the street and gable elevations of the house weighs 68 tonnes) is contrasted with larch cladding to the rear, to soften the garden elevation. The fabric and geometry of the building combine to make this structure a permanent marker and gateway to the site.

Continuity between architecture and landscape is something NORD always attempt to connect in their work. In this case, it takes on a more overt physical expression through the use of the Caithness stone, which roots the building to the site and locates the building in the wider landscape. The application of materiality also seeks to express a positive and meaningful relationship between architecture and landscape by various means, which go beyond the use of materials simply as decorative aspects of the building and site.

Materiality in this sense can be used to represent landscape and location in terms of how the materials of a given place result from natural ecological processes and cultural practices. As if excavated from the surrounding landscape, the stone, now reassembled on the buildings façades will appear like the dry stone walls found throughout Scotland.

CONSTRUCTION SYSTEM

Environmental impact was an important issue during the design process and this was explored to provide a sustainable approach to the construction and end use of the building. The super-insulated main structural elements were manufactured off site locally then delivered on site for a quick assembly. This 'timber frame' structure was then clad over in indigenous stone and timber. The house is insulated to a 'passive house' standard, using locally sourced materials where possible thus embracing the concept of 'sustainability'.

LESSONS LEARNED/KEY MESSAGES

We have drawn on vernacular forms, a long, low, one and a half storey terrace with an inhabited roof space, using indigenous materials and the specific landscape setting with its everyday and seasonal changes in colour, texture and light.

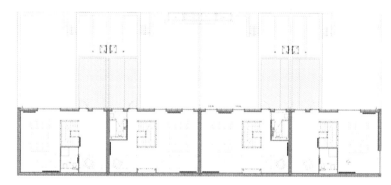

FIRST FLOOR

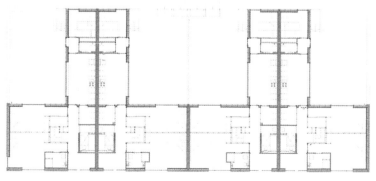

GROUND FLOOR

HOUSE NAME	The Stone House
ARCHITECT	NORD
CONTRACTOR	Robertson Highland
OWNER/ DEVELOPER	Highland Housing Alliance
HOUSE TYPE	Terrace of 4 houses
INTERNAL FLOOR AREA	Each house - 148m²
NUMBER OF BEDROOMS	3
NUMBER OF PUBLIC ROOMS	1 (open plan upper floor)
PREDICTED ANNUAL HEATING COST	£125
SAP RATING	
ENERGY USAGE (HEATING ONLY) IN kWh/m²	57 kWh/m²

FIGURE 1

FIGURE 2

FIGURE 3

FIGURE 4

FIGURE 5

FIGURE 6

PLOT 3   THE SHED HOUSE

The design for Plot 3 was particular to this site, a wider ambition for the project was to develop a model for affordable housing which had the potential to be applied to other sites. The simple four up/two down spatial arrangement makes maximum use of the building's foot print and contains the accommodation within a rectangular floor plan.

The final building's use of timber, slate and corrugated cement fibreboard express the same practical logic found in agricultural buildings in the region. Rather than dress our homes as castles, Plot 3 suggests the humble shed as a building form with more possibilities for building modern homes.

KEY DESIGN FEATURES

The orientation of the plot gave us the opportunity to open out the south-facing wall to take advantage of the sun path. Both the kitchen and living room have generous glazing to the garden. By reducing circulation space, the plan makes the most use of the building footprint. In addition, the ground floor could be adapted to accommodate bedroom space if required.

The houses have been designed using traditional timber frame technology. As well as providing scope for well-insulated, thermally efficient homes, timber frame offers a local 'buildability'. The frames were pre-fabricated off site locally and transportation of building parts was short. As a model for future projects, it was important for us to choose a construction type that maximised the potential to use the local work force. The external envelope of the buildings, is designed for minimal maintenance.

The building was simple to construct and offsite prefabrication resulted in a solution which we are confident will perform well in terms of energy efficiency based on a low technology solution.

CONSTRUCTION SYSTEM

The modern local building tradition for domestic buildings in the region is timber frame. The decision was made to use this form of construction as it offers flexibility for both the contractor and designer as well as being cost effective. The houses are constructed off an insulated concrete slab foundation, walls are a standard 100x50mm timber frame panels with 12mm plywood sheathing.

Mineral wool insulation is used to fill the void and additional rigid insulation is fixed to the inner line of the timber frame. The external cladding (untreated Scottish Larch/cement fibre board) is fixed to treated timber battens, which are nailed to the timber frame wall. Slates are nailed on to softwood sarking boards which are supported by timber trusses.

LESSONS LEARNED/KEY MESSAGES

The masterplan set out guidelines for the individual plot architects, who then pulled these together to produce a well-considered urban place. Unfortunately with most modern housing developments, this stage is often missing or is concerned with achieving only the objective of complying with vehicle access and parking.

The most valuable outcome of the Housing Expo as a whole has been the recognition that the creation of an enjoyable place to live requires urban planning on a larger scale, rather than piecemeal development. Overall masterplans can still offer enough flexibility to allow for individual house design to have variation and freedom.

In our view, it is in streets, avenues and parks that people prefer to live-out their lives, not characterless car-lined cul-de-sacs. The Expo has provided a model to test this theory.

FIRST FLOOR

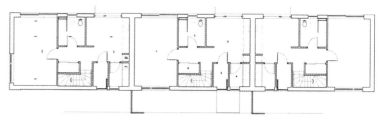

GROUND FLOOR

HOUSE NAME	The Shed House
ARCHITECT	The Highland Council
CONTRACTOR	Morrison Homes
OWNER/ DEVELOPER	Cairn Housing Association
HOUSE TYPE	Terrace of 3 houses
INTERNAL FLOOR AREA	Each house - 109m²
NUMBER OF BEDROOMS	4
NUMBER OF PUBLIC ROOMS	2
PREDICTED ANNUAL HEATING COST	£213
SAP RATING	B+
ENERGY USAGE (HEATING ONLY) IN kWh./²	119 kWh/m²

FIGURE 1

FIGURE 2

FIGURE 3

FIGURE 4

FIGURE 5

4.1 THE TIMBER HOUSE

The two houses are simple in plan, each making the most of the rear, south facing gardens and the view into the square and beyond. The corrugated aluminium cladding used on the roof and walls evokes the rural community hall designs found in the Highlands. This hard exterior encloses a softer interior with walls and ground floor ceiling all finished in exposed timber. The windows on the southern aspect are large, with patio doors opening into the private garden space, in order to maximise the benefits of passive solar gain. Additional skylight windows in the upstairs bedroom and hallway ensure there is plenty of daylight inside.

The houses are designed to be affordable and attractive to first time buyers. This has been achieved by keeping the layout simple and relying on the overall structure of the housing to bring a feeling of quality and spaciousness.

KEY DESIGN FEATURES

The design was driven by the site and limitations of the plot. The key design features result from the construction method and materials used, having solid timber walls and floors, a highly thermally efficient cassette roof (400mm glass fibre) and 200mm of wood fibre insulation applied to the external walls, all covered by corrugated aluminium cladding as well as a rendered board cladding. The exposure of the solid timber walls and ceiling in the living and dining areas (as well as upstairs) is a key feature. The timber introduces a feeling of warmth and as it is a hygroscopic material, internal humidity levels are managed and maintained to provide a comfortable atmosphere. The construction provides relatively high thermal mass, ensuring the house will retain heat in winter and will remain cool in summer.

The wall panels are engineered precisely, and site-assembled, making the construction very airtight. Party walls were also tested acoustically and achieved very good results.

For each of the two 2 bed houses, the solid timber construction 'locks-in' about 4.5 tonnes of carbon, helping to reduce the carbon footprint of the building.

CONSTRUCTION SYSTEM

The Timber House has 5 layer cross-laminated timber walls made from pieces of spruce and pine laid together across one another and bonded together to form a very strong 95mm thick panel. Using such a solid timber system to form the walls has great environmental benefits. Large pre-fabricated panels and simple construction mean that house walls can be erected up to roof level in a few days. Electrical wiring is dropped into small voids formed in the panel joints, allowing an uninterrupted, exposed finish to the timber walls and ceilings.

LESSONS LEARNED/KEY MESSAGES

Whilst the timber panels are pre-fabricated (by Martinsons's) in Sweden there is great potential for them to be made in Scotland from homegrown timber as we think this is a resource that could be used to greater effect. Protection of the timber panels during the wet weather is Scotland is essential as we had some 'capping' of the timber because of this.

The solid timber provides one hour fire resistance and was designed to act with a rainscreen cladding. We had proposed the use of intumescent fire breaks but Building Control insisted on fully filled fire breaks with additional vents above and below. We felt this was not appropriate to the type of cladding used. We did like the solid timber construction method and are using it on other projects.

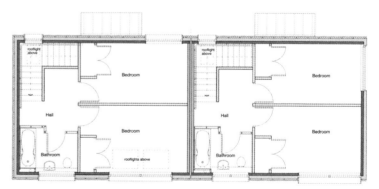

FIRST FLOOR

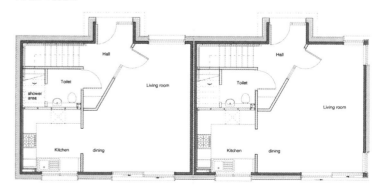

GROUND FLOOR

HOUSE NAME	The Timber House
ARCHITECT	John Gilbert Architects
CONTRACTOR	Morrison Homes
OWNER/ DEVELOPER	Albyn Housing Society
HOUSE TYPE	2 Semi-detached houses
INTERNAL FLOOR AREA	Each house - 78m²
NUMBER OF BEDROOMS	2
NUMBER OF PUBLIC ROOMS	2
PREDICTED ANNUAL HEATING COST	£73
SAP RATING	85 B
ENERGY USAGE (HEATING ONLY) IN kWh/m²	54 kWh/m²

FIGURE 1

FIGURE 2

FIGURE 3

FIGURE 4

FIGURE 5

The original concept behind 'The Healthy House' was to develop an exemplar for social housing by providing a healthy, sustainable and stimulating environment through flexible social spaces and visual links through double height spaces. The accomplishment of this was a considerable achievement, considering the restrictions of budget, economics and design briefs within social housing. The environmental agenda for the project was considered thoroughly with the above restrictions in mind. By adopting a common sense approach, avoiding the use of maintenance and energy hungry 'eco clichés', the scheme benefits from natural ventilation, passive solar gain and increased levels of insulation. The original concept provided a holistic approach to material choices to provide a healthy living environment; especially regarding the internal finishes such as natural clay paints, low toxicity carpets and natural stains/paints within a formaldehyde free construction. Due to budget restrictions these were omitted from the final construction, however the overall form and concept has been retained.

KEY DESIGN FEATURES

Following the original design concept of producing a high quality living environment through rational design, a number of simple but effective methods were adopted. Internally, the double height spaces allows a visual link between public spaces both upstairs and downstairs together with allowing good free air circulation through the building. This space also acts as a light well, bringing natural light into the depth of the plan. Adopting an open plan approach to the living spaces makes best use of the strict spatial limits required in social housing. The house was designed to take advantage of the plot orientation, maximising natural solar gain through the south westerly facing double height space, and assisted passive ventilation via prevailing westerly winds. Rooms were positioned to receive the best light suited to their function with smaller areas of glazing and non-habitable rooms to the rear offering privacy to the street.

CONSTRUCTION SYSTEM

The original concept design was based upon a breathing wall construction allowing a healthier internal air quality through the increased movement of air, assisted by the layering of non-toxic construction products such as timber cladding, steam compressed wood pulp boarding, recycled paper insulation, plaster board and clay paints. Due to strict budget requirements a number of changes were made while still remaining true to the original concept. A traditional timber frame construction was adopted which, although losing the breathing wall construction, allowed greater air tightness to be achieved. Low u-values were maintained in all main building elements (walls, floors, roofs, windows and doors).

LESSONS LEARNED/KEY MESSAGES

It was a difficult journey: balancing innovation, quality and performance with strict budget restrictions. The Healthy House demonstrates that it is possible to create a stimulating environment despite such restrictions. Arguably the original concept could be achieved if constructing more than two properties, through the benefits of the economy of scale. Nevertheless, the project has resulted in achieving an exemplar for modern social housing, while offering, financial, social and environmental benefits

FIRST FLOOR

GROUND FLOOR

HOUSE NAME	The Healthy House
ARCHITECT	Andrew Black Design
CONTRACTOR	William Gray Construction
OWNER/ DEVELOPER	Cairn Housing Association
HOUSE TYPE	2 Semi-detached houses
INTERNAL FLOOR AREA	Each house - 90m²
NUMBER OF BEDROOMS	3
NUMBER OF PUBLIC ROOMS	1
PREDICTED ANNUAL HEATING COST	£64
SAP RATING	B
ENERGY USAGE (HEATING ONLY) IN kWh/m²	117 kWh/m²

FIGURE 1

FIGURE 2

FIGURE 3

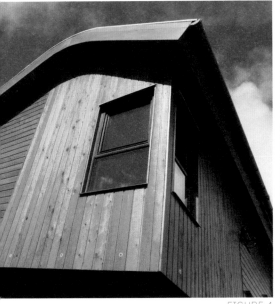

FIGURE 4

FIGURE 5

FIGURE 6

4.3

LIOS GORM (GREEN PLACE TO LIVE)

As a practice, we took a view that contemporary housing, whilst being technologically advanced in use of materials, design techniques and passive systems, should be simple in use. We have avoided the use of mechanical and user intensive devices to create a restful, versatile and instinctive environment in order to promote micro-community and personal well being. The advanced features of our houses are built-in, not bolted-on.

When considering the definition of domestic vernacular architecture, taking a historical new, it became apparent that this is a synthesis of the locally available building materials (limited by transport and cost considerations) and tried and tested construction techniques combined to create the best shelter possible. This approach drove the visual quality of vernacular architecture not the reverse. Therefore, we have avoided referencing conventional typologies and sought an honest visual expression of the materials, orientation and lifestyle that are relevant to the 21st century.

KEY DESIGN FEATURES

The design of Lios Gorm utilises modern methods of construction to minimise embodied energy and maximise quality. The roof, wall and floor cassettes were all manufactured under factory conditions and the pre-fabricated enhanced service cores designed to incorporate all of the electrical, water and ventilation systems. Off site construction minimises material and labour transportation, minimises waste, utilises efficient stock management techniques, maximises quality and minimises delays due to adverse weather.

The houses were designed to maximise solar gain from the south (framed construction with south west facing glazed infill) and minimise heat loss to the north (thick, well insulated walls with carefully selected to window penetrations). High embodied energy elements such as the concrete foundations and masonry substructure were minimised by offsetting them under the building by 500mm. In combination with the lightweight construction and single leaf support walls, the volume of concrete was reduced by 54%.

CONSTRUCTION SYSTEM

The factory made wall, floor and roof cassettes were formed in engineered timber JJI sections by James Jones and Sons with Warmcell cellulose fibre insulation to form breathing wall panels which we believe creates a healthier ambient living environment than the sealed envelope concept of conventional construction.

The engineered structural timber joists are formed from the waste of the primary Scottish timber industry and the external cladding is from the heartwood of locally sourced larch. A Passivent whole house ventilation is incorporated into pre-fabricated enhanced service cores and works on the natural stack effect without the need for mechanical extraction.

LESSONS LEARNED/KEY MESSAGES

We are now convinced that off-site construction is key to the future development of the Scottish building industry. It is integral to a truly sustainable procurement of volume and rural housing development. However, creative thinking from both the design and production sides of the industry will be required to allow progress to be made.

We also believe that costly 'eco technology' is not the answer to achieving sustainable housing with low running costs. Lios Gorm, with no 'green technology', equals and betters the performance figures of other low energy designed houses through careful design and specification and creates a restful home environment that promotes well being.

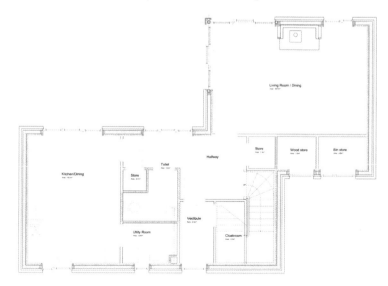

GROUND FLOOR

FIGURE 1

HOUSE NAME	Lios Gorm (Green Place to Live)
ARCHITECT	David Blaikie Architect
CONTRACTOR	William Gray Construction
OWNER/ DEVELOPER	Albyn Housing Society
HOUSE TYPE	2 storey house, upper flat and fully accessible lower flat
INTERNAL FLOOR AREA	2 storey house – 126m², upper flat – 52m²/lower flat – 52m²
NUMBER OF BEDROOMS	2 storey house – 3, upper flat – 1/lower flat – 1
NUMBER OF PUBLIC ROOMS	2 storey house – 2 ½, upper flat – 1/lower flat – 1
PREDICTED ANNUAL HEATING COST	2 storey house - £112, upper flat – £52/lower flat - £47
SAP RATING	83
ENERGY USAGE (HEATING ONLY) IN kWh/m²	house 37 kWh/m², upper 42 kWh/m², lower flat 39 kWh/m²

FIGURE 2

FIGURE 3

FIGURE 4

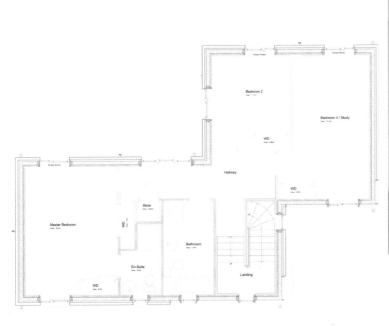

FIRST FLOOR

FIGURE 5

PLOT 5 THE CORNER HOUSE

Initially, the decision was made to look at Plot 5 as we felt that the position on site addressing the 'green' dealt with issues of privacy and formality on to this space. The plot is also on a corner and the highly visible nature of the house as you turn off the approach road we felt to be a design challenge as all sides of the house are clearly visible.

In addition to the factors above, we also liked the idea of designing a house that was part of a wall that could then become a live-work unit, creating a strong presence within the overall masterplan and would defining edges to create a protected and sheltered garden space.

KEY DESIGN FEATURES

Our interest in rural forms continues in the corner house both with the realisation that the house needs to respond to different viewpoints and perspectives within the site. An interest in occupying the roof volume is explored allowing for lower eaves heights but adding volumetric interest in the section.

The living space purposefully links the front of the house to the garden courtyard, giving both south and north light to the space. The living room is 'double height' with the study/small lounge space looking down from above.

The kitchen and dining space are adjacent to but not within the living space and set a half level below the garden. The house gable draws back from the wall allowing light to fall down into the kitchen. From the kitchen a path leads to the garden studio with niches in the wall allowing for the display of art and objects in the garden. The link wall between the house and studio acts as a windbreak creating a micro climate for growing plants and vegetables on what is essentially a hillside location.

Materially, the lower half of the house is built from handmade rustic bricks which have been laid in a variety of bonds to add further texture and visual interest to the wall.

CONSTRUCTION SYSTEM

The house is constructed from timber and bricks set on a highly insulated JJI timber frame construction. This allowed us to fold the roof like a mini landscape and to respond to the different site approaches.

The roof is clad in epdm (elastic damp-proof membrane) which allows us to achieve the unusual geometry. Using this system shortened the time of construction and helped to meet the tight Expo timescales.

LESSONS LEARNED/KEY MESSAGES

- Lessons Learned /key messages
- An exploration of a corner villa form
- The importance of internal space and roof form
- The flow of space from green to garden
- Top light to kitchen space
- The positive feeling of mixed north and south light
- The courtyard garden
- Volume in living space
- Low running costs
- Fast construction
- A home with identity

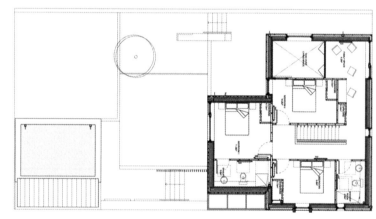

FIRST FLOOR

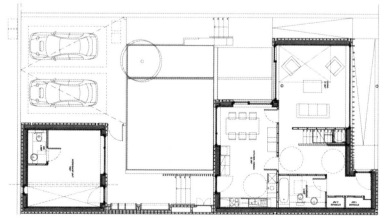

GROUND FLOOR

HOUSE NAME	The Corner House
ARCHITECT	JM Architects
CONTRACTOR	Robertson Highland
OWNER/ DEVELOPER	Highland Housing Alliance
HOUSE TYPE	Detached house with workshop
INTERNAL FLOOR AREA	House – 140m²
	Workshop - 22m²
NUMBER OF BEDROOMS	3
NUMBER OF PUBLIC ROOMS	2
PREDICTED ANNUAL HEATING COST	£136
SAP RATING	
ENERGY USAGE (HEATING ONLY) IN kWh/m²	107 kWh/m²

FIGURE 1

FIGURE 2

FIGURE 3

FIGURE 4

FIGURE 5

FIGURE 6

6 WOODROCK

Woodrock House is a contemporary, minimal living space split into two compositions of white and timber. These two boxes of 'honest industry' have penetrations into each skin to form balcony and window openings. This three-bedroom proposal house addresses its site location as a key element within the village hierarchy, commanding a position as the central focus of the proposed village green.

The common spaces within the house interlock with each other from gallery to living, kitchen and dining, encouraging unity, warmth and sharing. A double void links the main living area to the open first floor gallery. On the first floor, two of the three bedrooms access an external terrace that looks out over the village's green. The first floor layout could be easily reconfigured to provide a fourth bedroom.

KEY DESIGN FEATURES

The upper level of the house has random Trespa timber walnut panels in a 'Mondrian' arrangement that form an elevated timber enclosure. The ground floor is a mix of glass and white render wrapping around the house. These simple robust materials create a low maintenance, crisp contemporary aesthetic.

Spaces to the village green side of the house discreetly open from within on to this public space, in contrast with the private garden elevation with its open and transparent glazing. Garden and living areas share space via large connecting doors.

The house is open plan with a central void which traps solar heat and transfers it to a central masonry wall that provides storage in the form of thermal mass. Air-tight construction ensures minimal heat loss from unplanned air leakage and a highly insulated building fabric with a mechanical ventilation and heat recovery system ensures that tempered fresh air is constantly supplied to the spaces within.

CONSTRUCTION SYSTEM

The proposal is based on the "Passive House", a super-insulated, airtight system developed in Germany. Included in the solution are solar thermal panels, a cross flow heat exchanger providing a continuous flow of warmed or cooled filtered fresh air and low voltage lighting.

Timber frame construction is used to form the structure of the house. Cellulose insulation is blown between the studs and wood fibre cladding boards further insulate the internal spaces creating a wall construction with a U-value of 0.15W/m2 degC. The house is thermally efficient and economical to run.

LESSONS LEARNED/KEY MESSAGES

Sustainability must be considered as an integral part of the whole design. Energy efficiency is key when trying to reduce energy usage therefore the performance of the building envelope is crucial.

Due to the high initial cost and long pay back times relating to micro renewables, these should be used only as a supplement to natural passive design strategies. As such, consideration of building orientation and environmental management of internal spaces are fundamental to successful sustainable design.

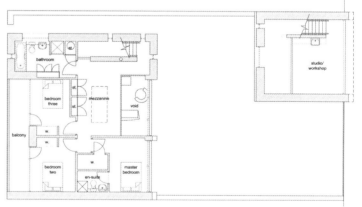

FIRST FLOOR

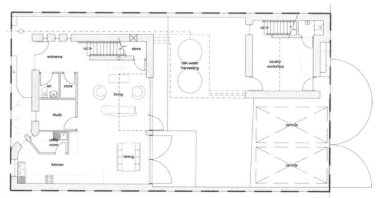

GROUND FLOOR

HOUSE NAME	Woodrock
ARCHITECT	AIM Design
CONTRACTOR	Robertson Highland
OWNER/ DEVELOPER	Highland Housing Alliance
HOUSE TYPE	Detached house with workshop
INTERNAL FLOOR AREA	House - 143m^2
	Workshop - 22m^2
NUMBER OF BEDROOMS	3
NUMBER OF PUBLIC ROOMS	1
PREDICTED ANNUAL HEATING COST	£322
SAP RATING	
ENERGY USAGE (HEATING ONLY) IN kWh/m^2	95 kWh/m^2

FIGURE 1

FIGURE 2

FIGURE 3

FIGURE 4

FIGURE 5

FIGURE 6

7 HOUSE No 7

This is a modest house designed to fit within a small almost urban site, including a garden car port and office work space in addition to the house itself. Three sides of the house open on to public space leading to an internalised layout of accommodation arranged round a central landscaped garden. Within these constraints the living areas of the house remain open to sun and views while retaining essential privacy where required. Internally, private areas – bedrooms, bathrooms, etc., are grouped around living areas at ground and first floor levels. Externally, robust materials have been deployed to reflect the semi-urban nature of the site, with precise detailing to achieve some delicacy in appearance.

KEY DESIGN FEATURES

A major factor in this design was the importance given to allowing free solar gains through south facing glazing to be utilised without incurring the problems of summer overheating. By grouping most cellular spaces such as bedrooms around the living areas, all free heat gains from the large south facing window are allowed to easily permeate the whole house and to be absorbed by the increased exposed surfaces. This is reinforced by a wall and floor construction that maximises the thermal mass exposed to these heat gains so allowing the building to respond dynamically to the benefits of the sun.

CONSTRUCTION SYSTEM

Thermal mass in the walls is achieved by constructing the external walls from two leaves of dense blockwork with 200mm insulation between. Carbon fibre wall ties were used and careful attention was paid to detailing of window openings to minimise cold bridging. Some steel framing was required to achieve the large glazed openings in the south elevation. The roof is constructed from 300mm JJI joists filled with insulation and lined externally with profiled metal sheeting. With reinforced concrete floors and both masonry and timber framed partitions internally the house is otherwise constructed normally. The attention to detail in the staircase and balustrading is significant in creating sense of quality as you move through the house.

LESSONS LEARNED/KEY MESSAGES

Clearly, the funding difficulties attached to the Expo had implications for the design and delivery of all of the houses. In our case the move to a design and build procurement method resulted in a difficult relationship with the contractor which was however largely overcome by the heroic contribution of their sub contractor who actually carried out most of the work and by the indestructible enthusiasm of the Highland Housing Alliance. We would undoubtedly wish to be involved in any future Housing Expo hopefully with a less tortuous method of delivery.

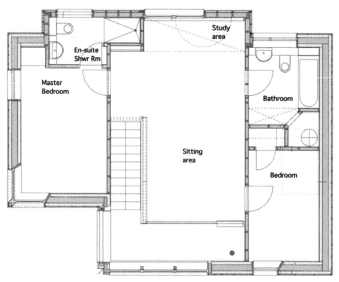

FIRST FLOOR

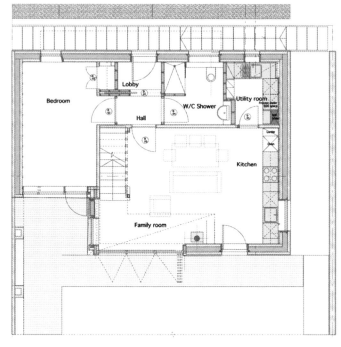

GROUND FLOOR

HOUSE NAME	House No 7
ARCHITECT	David Somerville Architects
CONTRACTOR	Robertson Highland
OWNER/ DEVELOPER	Highland Housing Alliance
HOUSE TYPE	Detached house with office
INTERNAL FLOOR AREA	124m²
NUMBER OF BEDROOMS	3
NUMBER OF PUBLIC ROOMS	2
PREDICTED ANNUAL HEATING COST	£146
SAP RATING	
ENERGY USAGE (HEATING ONLY) IN kWh/m²	62 kWh/m²

FIGURE 1

FIGURE 2
FIGURE 3
FIGURE 4

FIGURE 5
FIGURE 6

THE APARTMENTS

From the outset, we were aware that this was an entirely new and unique development, on a green field site. We were also conscious of respecting the relationships between our and the adjacent plots and infrastructure, frontage lines and issues associated with privacy and overlooking.

Our appraisal of the specific plot conditions inherent in the site masterplan layout led us to surmise that our response for the six affordable flats on Plot 8 must not only have a connection to Mews Court, but being the tallest building at the Expo, at three storeys, it must have a strong presence and identity on the site. From the briefing document, our solution was to be, **Robust** and **Urban** and a **Standalone**, **Landmark** building within the development.

KEY DESIGN FEATURES

The principle approach to the design was to take advantage of that which is free and maximise the use of passive strategies. We arranged the elements in such a manner as to allow the building to perform passively, reducing reliance on energy consumption for space heating and creating a regulated internal environment.

The Apartments are orientated to maximise solar benefits, both in terms of natural daylighting into the primary living spaces and passive solar gain, harnessed through the integral 'solar buffer space'. Collecting the sun's heat during the day, absorbing it in the thermal mass of the heavy masonry construction, and releasing the warmth into The Apartments at night. The fenestration patterns assist natural ventilation. The main living areas are predominantly open-plan to increase efficiency of space heating and flexibility of use. The thermal envelope far exceeds the current Building Standards.

All heating and hot water demands for the six apartments is provided through an independent biomass boiler located within the curtilage of the plot.

CONSTRUCTION SYSTEM

The majority of the building is constructed in a structural timber kit, with engineered members limited to floors where spans are required. For the external wall we developed a staggered twin stud arrangement, packed with cellulose insulation. Masonry construction was limited to areas in which it was required for either environmental performance in the form of thermal mass (solar buffer zone) or by the Building Standards (communal stair).

Most importantly, we have used understood construction techniques and commonly available materials. We have promoted appropriate and responsible sourcing of local materials, using reclaimed materials rather than new, wherever possible.

Our choice for the pallet used to create the aesthetic of the building was taken from the Expo Framework briefing document: 'Masonry and render providing the mute and monochrome appearance of natural building materials.'

LESSONS LEARNED/KEY MESSAGES

Replication of the units is fundamental to the Expo- this is not just a one-off showpiece, but a learning experience and we have maximised the opportunity for repeating the design - or at least the design principles, by developing an adaptable baseline solution that can be tailored towards any client's aspirations. However, any revisiting of the design must be carefully considered to suit specific site conditions and the performance of all systems, components and strategies must be integral to the design.

We stress that a key consideration is that we should at all times minimise energy reliance by maximising the use of that which is free, optimising construction performance and only then applying appropriate technologies. Through intensive analysis of design decisions, we have produced a pragmatic and responsible solution.

HOUSE NAME	The Apartments
ARCHITECT	Keppie Design
CONTRACTOR	William Gray Construction
OWNER/ DEVELOPER	Albyn Housing Society
HOUSE TYPE	6 Flats
INTERNAL FLOOR AREA	Each flat - 76m²
NUMBER OF BEDROOMS	2
NUMBER OF PUBLIC ROOMS	1
PREDICTED ANNUAL HEATING COST	£153 – 169
SAP RATING	86 - 87B
ENERGY USAGE (HEATING ONLY) IN kWh/m²	99 – 113 kWh/m²

FIGURE 1

FIGURE 2

FIGURE 3

FIGURE 4

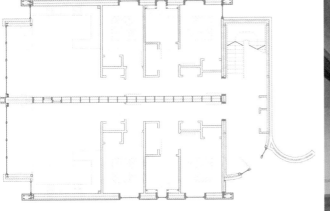

AL FLOOR PLAN

FIGURE 5

FIGURE 6

PLOT 9
THREE ON NINE

Three terraced houses were developed through the analysis of home, family and community within the Highland context. The project used simplicity and familiarity of the traditional terrace house as a starting point to respond directly to the site and surroundings to create a distinct sense of place.

Exploring the competition design code for the plot, which demanded a response that was 'lightweight and rural with emphasis on colour in the landscape' the concept of skin as a protector and weathering cover was the generator for the proposal. Taking a single natural material, treating it, running it into specific unit sizes and creating the built form focuses on the essential nature of timber as skin. Applying a light grey colour to harmonise the timber with the zinc roof gives an overall ethereal quality to the built form.

KEY DESIGN FEATURES

The design seeks to encourage social interaction between the houses through notional rather than physical boundaries, reflecting the Expo's ethos of creating and sustaining community. Thus with minimal excavation the houses step down the site following the contours of the land utilising natural drops to distinguish the boundaries between neighbours.

The roof is pitched as a traditional roof, but canted to the north to raise the building height on the south, thus maximising the southern aspect and giving a hierarchy to the internal spaces.

Large south-facing windows maximise solar gain and allow light deep into the plan supplemented by smaller north facing openings, reducing the need for artificial lighting. Manually controlled external blinds to the south and internal insulated shutters to all of windows were intended to assist with solar shading and heat loss. The section of the house was formed to enable cross ventilation and volumes of space.

CONSTRUCTION SYSTEM

A traditional timber kit system was used with critical adjustments in the main areas to create something of interest and joy. This approach was used to enable development of a house type that could be replicated throughout the UK while maintaining architectural and environmental ambitions. Each home employs a simple environmental strategy that provides well-lit healthy spaces incorporating a system of water recycling, heat recovery, solar water heating and an air source heat pump. Internally, the homes contain generously planned naturally lit spaces with a diversity of areas to inhabit.

Significant research was required for the timber cladding design to determine the most appropriate products available to us, while maintaining the material oneness of the scheme.

LESSONS LEARNED/KEY MESSAGES

We aimed to work closely with our developer client, who provided a series of filters, adding and subtracting from the original competition design entry. On reflection, further analysis between building costs and decisions made would better inform developments of the future.

We were fortunate to be one of only three plots selected by IKEA, the Swedish furnishing company, who fitted out all of the interiors of our houses demonstrating to the public the houses potential for differing user types/groups. We will continue to observe and learn from the richness of location and place and aim to develop appropriate contemporary architecture that is contextually rooted.

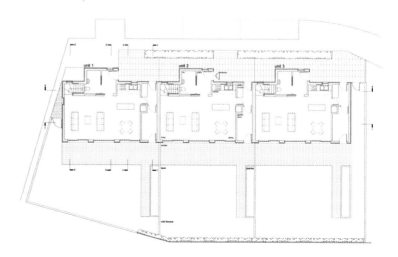

GROUND FLOOR

HOUSE NAME	Three on Nine
ARCHITECT	Graham Mitchell Architects
CONTRACTOR	William Gray Construction
OWNER/ DEVELOPER	Highland Housing Alliance
HOUSE TYPE	Terrace of 3 houses
INTERNAL FLOOR AREA	Each house - 110m^2
NUMBER OF BEDROOMS	3
NUMBER OF PUBLIC ROOMS	1
PREDICTED ANNUAL HEATING COST	£362
SAP RATING	73
ENERGY USAGE (HEATING ONLY) IN kWh/m^2	138 kWh/m^2

FIGURE 1

FIGURE 2

FIGURE 3

FIGURE 4

FIRST FLOOR

PLOT 10 — MASSIV PASSIV

The project designed for Plot 10 grew directly out of participation in an EU funded research project to investigate the relevance of massive timber systems to Scotland. The research took us to Austria where we studied leading-edge Austrian timber architecture. Economy of means, rigorous approach to energy conservation and concise timber detailing all inspired the design. It also reinforced a desire to experiment beyond the current vogue for reinterpretations of the traditional pitched roof form, risking a little more in visual terms and testing for ourselves the possibilities of the simplest of box shapes. Adopting this restraint seemed to us a critical part of our ongoing investigations of ecologically rigorous design and an aspect that under normal circumstances is hard to pursue both in response to Local Authority Planning and client pressures and expectations. The research project had already convinced us that massive timber systems offered unrivalled performance in terms of combined air tightness, thermal mass and carbon fixation together with exceptional speed of construction and raw, tactile, exposed internal timber surfaces that excite those with a love for surface and material.

KEY DESIGN FEATURES

The cross laminated timber panels form a complete structure of walls, roof and first floor with one structural partition. The majority of the panels are exposed internally to give a strong timber aesthetic. Almost all of the components used are solid timber and the provenance of this timber restricted to known sources, evaluated in relation to good forestry practice. External cladding, flooring and all internal finishings were specified in Scottish timber, the design team having a long track record in the procurement and specification of such material. Insulation – applied externally to give exceptional air tightness – is wood fibre from European sources. The roof however is insulated in local straw bales. When insulation as deep as 300mm is required, this is an ideal material and the flat roof would allow particularly easy installation. The majority of the south elevation of each house is glazed to provide high solar gain and daylighting – moderated by internal, sliding timber louvres and an unenclosed staircase. The spatial design is deliberately compact yet offers a spacious living space with daylight from both south and north. Space and water heating by wood pellet stove utilises locally produced fuel from certified forests, stimulating reforestation.

CONSTRUCTION SYSTEM

Cross laminated timber panels (spruce and fir) imported from Austria and crane erected by Eurban Ltd (London & Inverness) an engineering and construction company specialising in this type of construction. Insulated externally with wood fibreboards on the walls and local straw bales in the roof. Solid concrete ground floor. Walls clad in local timber and roof covering a single ply membrane. Floors and finishings solid home-grown hardwood.

LESSONS LEARNED/KEY MESSAGES

As the project was not built, the outcome for us as a design team relates only to the design and procurement process. This only reinforced previous experience that the way buildings are procured - and especially innovative ones – is critical.

At the invitation of the client, Eurban/North Woods tendered this project on budget and could easily have delivered it, both companies being designer/builders. However, the client maintained that their developer's tender, although £100k higher, was their preferred route.

Subsequently the project was declared unfundable. A lack of transparency in the procurement and tendering process left us dissatisfied with the explanations we received.

FIRST FLOOR

GROUND FLOOR

SCOTLAND'S HOUSING EXPO 2010 · CHAPTER 6 · THE EXPO AS BUILT · PAGE 92

FIGURE 1

HOUSE NAME	Massiv Passiv
ARCHITECT	North Woods/Locate Architects with Eurban
CONTRACTOR	Not appointed
OWNER/ DEVELOPER	Highland Housing Alliance
HOUSE TYPE	Terrace of 3 houses
INTERNAL FLOOR AREA	Each house - 95m2
NUMBER OF BEDROOMS	2
NUMBER OF PUBLIC ROOMS	1
PREDICTED ANNUAL HEATING COST	£287
SAP RATING	76 C
ENERGY USAGE (HEATING ONLY) IN kWh/m²	32 kWh/m2

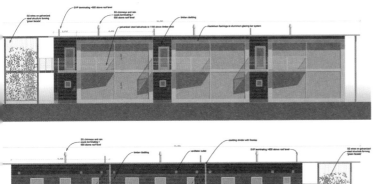

FIGURE 2

In going beyond current UK best practice and setting a new benchmark for low energy residential design in Scotland and the UK, HLM Architect's concept for the 3 terraced houses on Plot 11, takes on the rigorous German 'PassivHaus' standard for energy efficiency. Translated to the Scottish context, this has resulted in three of ultra low-energy houses, which dispense with conventional heating systems altogether. The heating load is so small in these dwellings that in theory a hairdryer could be used to heat the house.

We felt it important to design a series of houses which were quiet, modest and contextual but with a progressive and innovative response to the Expo's sustainability aspirations: housing that would also be affordable and attractive to both volume house builders and social housing providers alike.

KEY DESIGN FEATURES

Our certified Passive House terrace, has achieved an 80% reduction in energy demand compared with regulation requirements through careful orientation and a compact form, using a locally manufactured off-site prefabricated closed panel system which along with high performance triple glazed windows, provide a super insulated air–tight building fabric. The result is a massive reduction in ventilation heat losses whilst ensuring excellent thermal comfort internally. A balanced mechanical ventilation system with heat recovery is also employed as a key element of the strategy, not only reducing heating bills but also providing a continuous supply of clean, fresh, excellent quality air. Hot water is provided from an air source heat pump located in the back garden. Enhanced biodiversity is provided through careful landscape design and the use of local species.

CONSTRUCTION SYSTEM

The dwellings utilise a locally manufactured PassiveWall™ timber panel system for wall, floor and roof elements. Manufactured off site, the system helps ensure a high standard of construction quality and accuracy, providing extremely low U-values and exceptional levels of air tightness. The panels utilise predominantly home grown Scottish timber, and contain a locally manufactured insulated core of recycled content glass wool insulation.

The panels are wrapped with a thermal foil membrane and internally with a thermal vapour barrier which provides the main air tight seal.

Externally the units are clad in a home grown untreated Scottish larch which will be left to weather naturally to a silver grey colour, embedding the buildings within the landscape.

LESSONS LEARNED/KEY MESSAGES

Plot 11 has been a test bed for building to Passive House standards in the Scottish climate, with local materials and local expertise. However, following the successful build process and the Expo event itself together with our client body and contractor, we now have the confidence, skill base and expertise to build to this ultra low energy standard here in Scotland. It is our intention that the 3 houses will be monitored over a 12-18 month period: thus comparing the habits, living styles and energy usage of three different families. It is only from this that we will learn the real lessons of the Expo – when the site becomes a living, breathing, community.

We think there is a genuine future for Passive House in mainstream housing, both social and private, and our challenge now is to deliver Passive House as an affordable solution to mass market housing.

FIRST FLOOR

GROUND FLOOR

HOUSE NAME	The Passive House
ARCHITECT	HLM Architects
CONTRACTOR	O'Brien Homes
OWNER/ DEVELOPER	Highland Housing Alliance
HOUSE TYPE	Terrace of 3 houses
INTERNAL FLOOR AREA	Each house - 107m²
NUMBER OF BEDROOMS	3
NUMBER OF PUBLIC ROOMS	1
PREDICTED ANNUAL HEATING COST	£107
SAP RATING	B
ENERGY USAGE (HEATING ONLY) IN kWh/m²	14 kWh/m²

FIGURE 1

FIGURE 2

FIGURE 3

FIGURE 4

FIGURE 5

FIGURE 6

In designing the Gem we have endeavoured to demonstrate that the competition sustainability targets for the project could be achieved in a manner that is attractive, homely and affordable, so that these exemplar standards can be achievable for all future housing. The Gem is one of the few houses in the Expo that survived the recession in the originally intended funding model as a privately funded house for sale, and it was one of the first to be sold.

The Gem is a distinctive super-insulated reinterpretation of a Highland cottage constructed of locally sourced indigenous materials, bright and cosy with generous south facing windows.

KEY DESIGN FEATURES

The house is based on passive solar principles with generous south facing rooms. This is achieved with a very efficient circulation core, located on the north side and a simple building profile and layout that allows the whole volume to be maximised and used efficiently to create a house with rooms that feel spacious, bright and airy.

The living, dining and kitchen areas are located on the first floor, allows them to benefit from the spectacular views over Inverness to the Beauly Firth and the mountains beyond. These rooms have a ceiling that is open to the rafter line with south facing windows and roof lights, making them very spacious and bright. They open to small balconies supported on projecting roof trusses, which combine to give the house its distinctive appearance.

The home office is integrated within the ground floor of the main house, allowing more flexibility so that the office can be used as a fourth bedroom or family room if preferred.

CONSTRUCTION SYSTEM

The house is highly energy efficient. The roof, walls and floors are insulated to a standard approximately 60% higher than the 2007 Building Regulation requirements. This is achieved with an innovative double stud and rafter arrangement, which allows more insulation and reduces the risk of cold bridges. The house is well draught proofed, which together with well controlled ventilation allows the house to achieve further energy efficiency.

The internal partitions and floors are masonry to help store passive heat gains and spread the benefit over 24 hours.

The house has generously sized solar panels and a large hot water buffer storage tank, so that for much of the year these will provide the bulk of the hot water and space heating requirements of the house, backed up by an air source heat pump, and log stove.

LESSONS LEARNED/KEY MESSAGES

For a small rural practice, the time and effort that went into this project is immense, and will never be reflected in any financial return on the project. In our view, much of that was due to the bureaucracy of the organisation of the Expo. If such an event is repeated it must find a format that allows the architects and their builders get on with it.

However, the over-riding experience of taking part in the Expo was absolutely positive. We spent some time in our house during the Expo, meeting the visitors and the positive feed back we received was tremendous. Reaction to the house, and the Expo generally, was almost entirely good, and when we were able to discuss and explain design issues with visitors this was extremely well received and mutually beneficial.

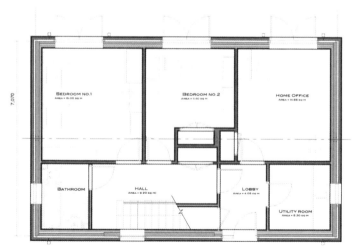

GROUND FLOOR

HOUSE NAME	The Gem
ARCHITECT	Trevor Black Architects
CONTRACTOR	O'Brien Homes
OWNER/ DEVELOPER	O'Brien Homes
HOUSE TYPE	Detached house
INTERNAL FLOOR AREA	143m²
NUMBER OF BEDROOMS	3
NUMBER OF PUBLIC ROOMS	2
PREDICTED ANNUAL HEATING COST	£96
SAP RATING	86
ENERGY USAGE (HEATING ONLY) IN kWh/m²	23 kWh/m²

FIGURE 1

FIGURE 2

FIGURE 3

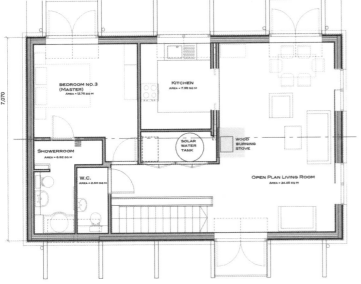

FIRST FLOOR

BEDROOM NO.3 (MASTER)
AREA = 12.75 SQ M

KITCHEN
AREA = 7.36 SQ M

SHOWERROOM
AREA = 6.62 SQ M

W.C.
AREA = 2.60 SQ M

SOLAR WATER TANK

WOOD BURNING STOVE

OPEN PLAN LIVING ROOM
AREA = 34.45 SQ M

7.070

FIGURE 4

FIGURE 5

14 THE SKYLIGHT HOME

The overall design intent for the house on Plot 14 was to create a building simple in external form, yet internally spatially dynamic, using innovative materials and construction to provide a sustainable and highly energy conscious building.

The design is an 'upside down' house, with the main living spaces deliberately placed on the first floor in order to make the most of the available roof volume and potential for natural light. A large roof light running along the ridge of living, dining and kitchen spaces provides a large amount of natural light, for a relatively small amount of glazing.

KEY DESIGN FEATURES

The house is a healthy, breathing home. It is timber framed with the primary innovative energy feature being the use of a dynamic breathing permeable insulated roof. This system allows fresh air for the house to be provided by an innovative 'Dynamic Breathing Building' system that allows pre-treated air to pass through special insulation cells in the roof. The air is supplied directly to the indoor living spaces of the house, replacing moist, stale air that is exhausted via an exhaust air heat pump providing fresh warm air in the winter and cool air in the summer. The Energyflo cells also filter particulate matter from the air entering the house.

The feature ridge skylight provides a natural light to the main living space of the house, reducing the use of artificial lights. Heating is provided by the exhaust air heat pump and radiators. A small wood burning stove also features in the design.

CONSTRUCTION SYSTEM

The primary structure of the building is an FSC certified timber frame. The timber frame is insulated (both walls and roof) with high performing 'energy flo cells', in lieu of a traditional insulating material.

The house also features an exhaust air heat pump, working much like an air source heat pump but instead of taking air from outside this works internally, by taking heat from exhaust air from toilets, utility areas and kitchens. This system pre-heats up water before it enters the boiler which tops up the heat if required.

All materials and building elements, where possible, were sourced from local suppliers, with Scottish larch being used extensively in the external cladding of the building.

LESSONS LEARNED/KEY MESSAGES

The building in its completed design form, without the use of any 'wacky' design features, begins to demonstrate the potential for improved energy performance over a house of 'traditional' layout and construction. This potential hopefully encourages and suggests a model for future housing design and development.

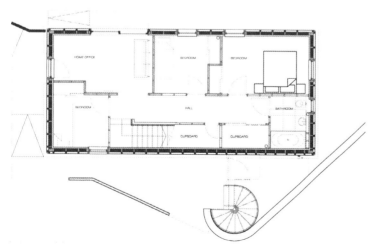

GROUND FLOOR

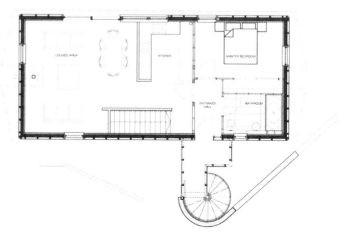

FIRST FLOOR

HOUSE NAME	The Skylight Home
ARCHITECT	Richard Murphy Architects
CONTRACTOR	Tulloch Homes Express
OWNER/ DEVELOPER	Highland Housing Alliance
HOUSE TYPE	Detached house
INTERNAL FLOOR AREA	134m²
NUMBER OF BEDROOMS	4
NUMBER OF PUBLIC ROOMS	2
PREDICTED ANNUAL HEATING COST	£279
SAP RATING	
ENERGY USAGE (HEATING ONLY) IN kWh/m²	27 kWh/m²

FIGURE 1

FIGURE 2

FIGURE 3

FIGURE 4

FIGURE 5

FIGURE 6

PLOT 15

THE MODULAR HOUSE

Bracewell Stirling Architects (now Consulting) is a long established practice with offices in Tillicoultry and Inverness. The practice has been designing predominantly housing in the Highlands and Inverness area for over 20 years. Much of this has been developer-led and our long established client, Tulloch Homes are our partners in the design and production of Plot 15. As a team, we saw this as an exciting opportunity to create a dwelling to meet the specific plot brief. The aim was to create a design with ground breaking thermal performance using modular construction based on factory assembly, which could be rolled out to the mass private housing market – consequently raising the standard of all housing and putting such solutions within the reach of all house buyers. The house is unique as it was originally designed with a developer whose intention was to test an entirely new approach to construction in terms of applicability to mainstream housing.

KEY DESIGN FEATURES
Ground breaking thermal performance & heating system

- Scotframe Supawall with injected insulation system
  Air tight/rigid/fairly lightweight vs thermal performance/ reduced bulk vs maximum thermal performance
- Wall U-value 0.11 W/m2degC compared with required 0.3/2.5 in Expo brief
- High performance window 0.8 W/m2degC compared with Regulation of 1.8
- Roof 0.1 W/m2degC compared with traditional of 0.2
- Heat pump chosen to be future proof/avoid dependence on fossil fuels. Type chosen to recycle air from wet areas to maximise efficiency.

Modular construction with factory assembly (not to be confused with pre-fabrication.

- Long panel construction with service zone all windows and doors prefitted
- Minimise on-site period to wind and water tight to fraction of normal timescales
- Controlled factory assembly means more control of construction quality
- Less material waste/less waste for landfill and less transport to and from site
- Almost nil exposure of materials to the weather creating less defects like shrinkage

- Like car assembly line would allow standardisation of service installations/kitchens /bathrooms creating less defects.

CONSTRUCTION SYSTEM
Factory assembled long closed panel construction using Supawall timber kit as base with pre-fitted service zone, windows and doors prefitted.

'Nibe' Exhaust Air Heat Pump with underfloor heating and radiators.

LESSONS LEARNED/KEY MESSAGES
We were in the unique position that our house was originally designed with the developer and so it was realistic in terms of incorporating design features for the user rather than a 'catwalk creation'. The approach adopted – providing practical living spaces for the modern family proved popular with the public. The process demonstrated that there is more to sustainability than renewables, with 'eco bling' taking second place to enhancement of the building fabric in order to minimise heating demand. The adopted approach also reduced waste and embodied energy and instigated the processes required to achieve this. It highlighted the potential for extending the off site manufacturing and assembly elements of the construction process.

GROUND FLOOR

FIGURE 1

HOUSE NAME	The Modular House
ARCHITECT	Bracewell Stirling Architects
CONTRACTOR	Tulloch Homes Express
OWNER/ DEVELOPER	Tulloch Homes Express
HOUSE TYPE	Detached house with office
INTERNAL FLOOR AREA	169m²
NUMBER OF BEDROOMS	4
NUMBER OF PUBLIC ROOMS	3
PREDICTED ANNUAL HEATING COST	£290
SAP RATING	74
ENERGY USAGE (HEATING ONLY) IN kWh/m²	102 kWh/m²

FIGURE 2

FIGURE 3

FIRST FLOOR

FIGURE 4

16 WHITE HOUSE

This house takes its name from the all over resin-based sprayed white coating, which references the distinctive whitewashed buildings found throughout the Scottish Highlands. It seeks to develop a spatial language appropriate to the Highlands in the twenty-first century, and to displace the perception of sustainable housing: replacing that of 'alternative' technology with that of expressive architectural space and form with integrated technology.

KEY DESIGN FEATURES

The layout reverses that of the typical suburban home, with living accommodation on the upper level and bedrooms located below.

The partitioned lower floor, accommodating entrance hall, three bedrooms and two bathrooms, forms a rigid structural base, allowing the formation of a large open plan arrangement of living spaces above to take advantage of distant views. A skew in plan, to comply with the frontage requirements of the stipulated design code, leads to a spatial distortion and an asymmetric roof form spanning the entire upper level. Within this space sit two objects – kitchen and stair – which loosely subdivide the large volume into smaller areas. In conjunction with stair and kitchen, the placement of windows leads to a dynamic, rotational spatial quality.

CONSTRUCTION SYSTEM

The White House utilises the properties of multiplan cross laminated timber panels manufactured by Mayr-Melnhof Kaufmann in Austria. The panels are typically around 3m wide by up to 12.1m in length and in thicknesses of 140mm, 163mm and 220mm as required. They are exposed in the house interior and were consequently specified with a visible furniture grade finish with service runs pre-routed into the panels in the factory. The timber structure is externally insulated and clad with fibre cement panels with a white resin-based spray applied waterproof finish to both walls and roof.

LESSONS LEARNED/KEY MESSAGES

The use of the cross laminated timber panel system has been successful with a minimum on-site construction period for the structure, good quality robust, internal finish and inherent sustainable credentials.

The upper level living space is spatially dynamic and its scale and openness should work well with current modes of family living.

We believe that the project demonstrates a sensible, economic approach to developing a low energy home, based on passive measures and a high performance envelope.

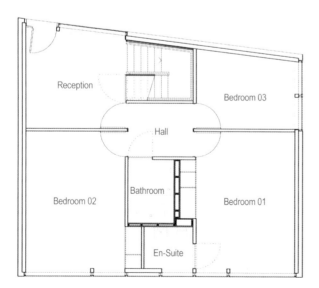

GROUND FLOOR

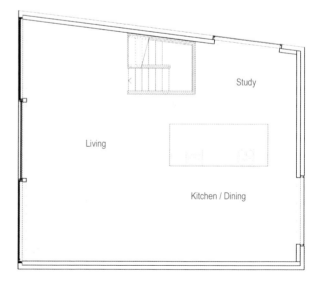

FIRST FLOOR

HOUSE NAME	White House
ARCHITECT	Graeme Massie Architects
CONTRACTOR	O'Brien Homes
OWNER/ DEVELOPER	Highland Housing Alliance
HOUSE TYPE	Detached house
INTERNAL FLOOR AREA	155m²
NUMBER OF BEDROOMS	3
NUMBER OF PUBLIC ROOMS	1 (open plan upper floor)
PREDICTED ANNUAL HEATING COST	£158
SAP RATING	83
ENERGY USAGE (HEATING ONLY) IN kWh/m²	63 kWh/m²

FIGURE 1

FIGURE 2

FIGURE 3

FIGURE 4

17 THE SECRET GARDEN

The Secret Garden was designed to reflect the location of the architects, Rural Design who are based on the north western edge of the Isle of Skye, one of the most remote parts of the UK. On the island, there is a tradition of crofting and the need for shelter has created walled gardens, within which an oasis of growth is cultivated in an otherwise barren landscape. The way of life on Skye has been mirrored in the design of the house. Rural Design are keen that the sustainability theme should be reflected not only in the house design, but in the lifestyle which it suggests.

KEY DESIGN FEATURES

The house sits within a walled garden in which the future occupants will be able to grow their own fruit and vegetables, promoting self sufficiency and organic gardening. The garden dictates the organisation of the house. The south facing side enjoys the most natural light and houses the kitchen and dining area, with the whole food process (growing, making and eating) taking place in the same area. On the south side is the living room, looking out on to the recreational part of the garden.

CONSTRUCTION SYSTEM

As is common for west-coast buildings (on account of the high winds) the house does not feature any overhanging eaves or unnecessary projections, and has a 'clipped' look. The house uses all of the space available to maximum effect, with every square mm used. Sleeping platforms sit within the roof volume, freeing up floor space for other uses. The architects believe in promoting heat conservation rather than the installation of ecogadgets, an approach commonly known as 'eco-minimalism'. To promote this, the walls are twice the thickness of normal construction, most of the heat required will be produced by a woodburning stove in the living room supported by the high levels of insulation and a scheme of whole house ventilation with heat recovery. High specification windows have been used, with a heat loss coefficient that means they are twice as efficient as that which would normally be used. The primary material used is timber, as locally sourced as possible, which reduces the overall carbon footprint of the house. All other materials used are completely recyclable where possible.

LESSONS LEARNED/KEY MESSAGES

The house itself is a modern reinterpretation of the character of houses found on Skye, which over the years have been added to and extended. Evoking this Highland tradition, the house includes a lean-to – a deliberate addition to the main house. This space allows the living room to enjoy a high ceiling, and a large rooflight brings south light right into the heart of the house.

FIRST FLOOR

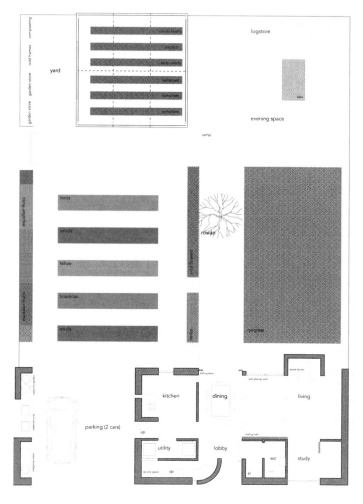

GROUND FLOOR

HOUSE NAME	The Secret Garden
ARCHITECT	Rural Design
CONTRACTOR	James Macqueen Building Contractor ltd
OWNER/ DEVELOPER	Highland Housing Alliance
HOUSE TYPE	Detached house
INTERNAL FLOOR AREA	137m²
NUMBER OF BEDROOMS	3
NUMBER OF PUBLIC ROOMS	2
PREDICTED ANNUAL HEATING COST	£320
SAP RATING	
ENERGY USAGE (HEATING ONLY) IN kWh/m²	126 kWh/m²

FIGURE 1

FIGURE 2

FIGURE 3

FIGURE 4

FIGURE 5

FIGURE 6

18

THE WHOLE LIFE HOUSE

The whole life house has been designed for the long term, to change and adapt to the complex ways that families now live and work. The design enables the house to be used for a number of different purposes, working with the life cycle of a family. It aim is to enable the occupants to choose to stay in the house rather than having the cost and upheaval of moving to another property.

The house features a separate ground floor annexe, which can be adapted for use as a granny flat, student bedsit, or provide additional bedroom space for a growing family. Alternatively the annexe could be used as a home office, providing separation between home life and work.

KEY DESIGN FEATURES

In the Whole Life House the kitchen and living room have been designed as the heart of the home, with exposed timber beams to the ceiling and large south facing windows to the garden, with working shutters. The open plan kitchen and living room are partially screened by integrated shelving to enable each space to have a distinct individual character.

A dramatic double height sunspace is accessed from the living room, and leads directly out into the garden. This bright sunny room provides additional living space whilst also allowing the property to benefit from the heat generated by direct solar gain. In the cold winter months the sunspace can be closed off from the living room, to prevent heat loss.

The property also benefits from having a highly insulated building shell, thermal mass solid ground floor, solar thermal panels for hot water and under-floor heating.

CONSTRUCTION SYSTEM

Walls consist of a timber kit system tightly packed with insulation, and a further insulated internal service zone. The external wall finish is a mix of rendered concrete block and Scottish larch cladding.

The ground floor is solid concrete with embedded under floor heating pipes, finished in large recycled porcelain slabs.

The first floor structure is formed with exposed glulam beams with redwood lining boards similar to the ceiling finish to the living room and kitchen.

The roof structure is a conventional timber kit truss, finished with zinc metal sheeting.

LESSONS LEARNED/KEY MESSAGES

The key lesson from the whole life house is flexibility. Families today are complex and house building needs to reflect this. People need homes that can adapt and change as their family circumstances change. Houses need to provide the scope for home working, growing families and live-in relatives.

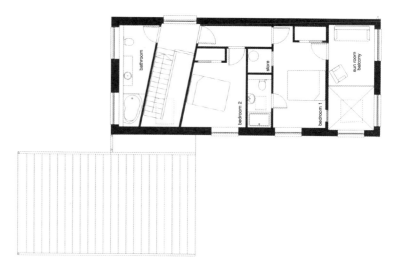

FIRST FLOOR

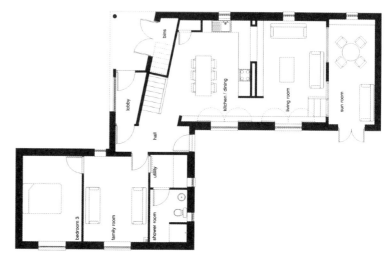

GROUND FLOOR

HOUSE NAME	The Whole Life House
ARCHITECT	Brennan and Wilson Architects
CONTRACTOR	Tulloch Homes Express
OWNER/ DEVELOPER	Highland Housing Alliance
HOUSE TYPE	Detached house
INTERNAL FLOOR AREA	165m²
NUMBER OF BEDROOMS	3 (with potential for 4)
NUMBER OF PUBLIC ROOMS	3 (including sunspace)
PREDICTED ANNUAL HEATING COST	£132
SAP RATING	83 B
ENERGY USAGE (HEATING ONLY) IN kWh/m²	46 kWh/m²

FIGURE 1

FIGURE 2

FIGURE 3

FIGURE 4

FIGURE 5

FIGURE 6

19 TWIN PEAKS

The Plot 19 house at Scotland's Housing Expo is a reinterpretation of Scottish rural vernacular buildings. By splitting the house into two distinct, offset volumes a larger footprint was achieved whilst maintaining the proportion of familiar 6m wide gable-ended volumes found throughout the Scottish countryside.

Each volume has a distinct character: a 'closed' white rendered north elevation serves as an environmental buffer whilst giving privacy to the occupants and an 'open' timber clad south elevation provides maximum passive solar gain and a direct connection with the garden.

The living, dining and cooking spaces on the ground floor plan are arranged around a south facing landscaped courtyard, reinforcing the connection between the inside living spaces and the garden. A double-height living volume serves as the focus of the house, linking ground and first floor rooms whilst permitting an abundance of direct southern sunlight into the heart of the home.

KEY DESIGN FEATURES
The design was inspired by the need to provide a sustainable house without using bolt-on technologies that a growing family could live in with ease and flexibility. The overriding emphasis of the design was to keep the spatial organisation simple. Two rectangles form the basis of a straightforward plan and a double height living volume anchors the section. By shifting the rectangles in plan, two positively defined external spaces are created: an entrance court to the north and a garden court to the south.

The ground floor accommodation is based on an open plan layout around the south facing garden court. The upper floor accommodation contains the bedrooms. A straight run stair, situated along the intersection of the two rectangles, separates the parents' sleeping domain from the other rooms. The pitch of the roof is articulated in the upper floor rooms, providing a relief from the traditional flat ceiling. The organisation of fenestration in relation to the accommodation is designed to take maximum advantage of passive solar gain.

The ground floor slab is exposed to sunlight and thus provides a degree of radiant heat at night and the double height living volume and position of the stair encourage passive movement of warm air throughout the house. Should the occupants desire additional accommodation, the living volume is designed to accommodate the insertion of a floor plate without disturbing the external envelope.

CONSTRUCTION SYSTEM
The structure comprises a prefabricated timber frame superstructure capped with prefabricated timber scissor trusses supported on in-situ concrete foundations. The external envelope is a light weight, highly insulated structure. The concrete ground floor slab provides thermal mass to help mediate the effects of solar gain. The external walls are wrapped in a proprietary insulated render system without the need for a traditional cavity. This provides the timber frame wall structure with a continuous thermal skin. The roof is clad in standing seam zinc for longevity and the scissor truss roof void is highly insulated.

LESSONS LEARNED/KEY MESSAGES
By keeping the design and detailing simple, the house was built to budget without compromising the spatial layout. Many visitors appreciated the qualities of the light filled airy internal spaces. In fact, some visitors liked the house so much that they have commissioned a 'Twin Peaks' for their own plot. Joseph Thurrott architects is presently designing a 'Twin Peaks' to Passivhaus standard for a client on the west coast of Scotland.

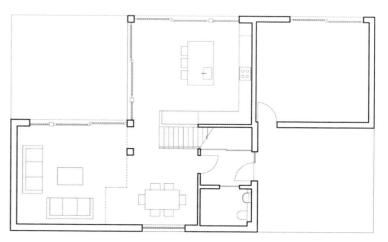

GROUND FLOOR

HOUSE NAME	Twin Peaks
ARCHITECT	Joseph Thurrott Architects
CONTRACTOR	Tulloch Homes Express
OWNER/ DEVELOPER	Highland Housing Alliance
HOUSE TYPE	Detached house
INTERNAL FLOOR AREA	150m²
NUMBER OF BEDROOMS	4
NUMBER OF PUBLIC ROOMS	1 (open plan ground floor)
PREDICTED ANNUAL HEATING COST	£435
SAP RATING	81 B
ENERGY USAGE (HEATING ONLY) IN kWh/m²	125 kWh/m²

FIGURE 1

FIGURE 2

FIGURE 3

FIGURE 4

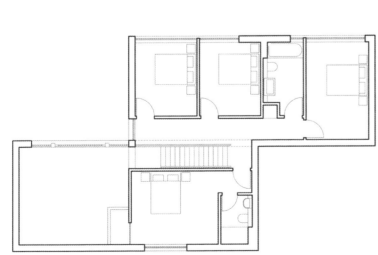

FIRST FLOOR

FIGURE 5

20 PLOT 20

Keppie Design have taken a simple, traditional and sustainable ethos and adapted it for current construction methods to create a contemporary home with exceptional thermal performance. We believe we have achieved a comfortable home with commonly used house building features that appeal to the wider market, while incorporating key sustainable elements.

The orientation of the dwelling maximises the opportunities for passive solar heating and natural ventilation. Simple sustainable design features have been incorporated such as cycle storage to provide and encourage alternatives to car usage. There is a large garden with ample natural hard and soft landscaping, space for a vegetable garden and an external drying area.

KEY DESIGN FEATURES

The design worked within the parameters of the master plan to define the street edge without compromising the orientation of the building to maximise passive solar benefits.

We have utilised enhanced methods of thermal performance by heavily insulating the external walls, roof and floor. To provide further warmth and additional external sound insulation, we specified composite triple glazed windows, ensuring maximum energy efficiency throughout the building, with key features such as low-emissivity coatings being added to the glass to further avoid valuable heat escaping.

The internal design was well-received as the Scottish Housing Expo progressed thanks to a 'traditional homely feel', complimented by bright and open spaces. The main reception rooms all maximise the benefits of a south facing view.

A wood burning stove has been installed, contributing towards heating the house locally at ground floor level, helping add to the traditional features of the house, along with its authentically designed surround.

CONSTRUCTION SYSTEM

The house utilises a common method of construction, enhanced to allow increased levels of insulation and to create an extremely thermally efficient building envelope, aiding the reduction in energy consumption and running costs.

A timber frame construction containing high performance rigid urethane insulation boards, which achieve a BRE Green Guide A Rating, have been used together with protective and decorative larch cladding in-part. A naturally strong and durable material, which was been locally and responsibly sourced.

To weatherproof the majority of the dwelling, a textured dry dash render has been applied to compliment our common house build approach.

LESSONS LEARNED/KEY MESSAGES

Keppie Design considers a modern, yet traditional and comfortable home can be achieved by focusing on current and well-practised methods of construction. We also learned that passive methods of heating and ventilation are valuable as a natural, essentially free and extremely effective resource when a dwelling is designed to maximise their use. All of this helped prove to us there can be little need for more expensive technologies if the house design is well considered through correct orientation and internal space planning. This was our primary focus and we believe we have maximised this in our finished home.

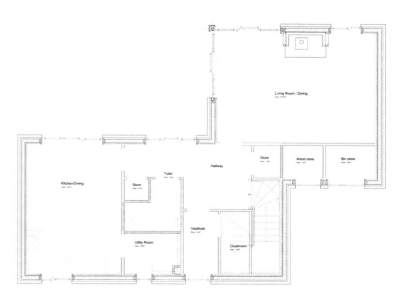

GROUND FLOOR

HOUSE NAME	Plot 20
ARCHITECT	Keppie Design
CONTRACTOR	Robertson Highland
OWNER/ DEVELOPER	Robertson Highland
HOUSE TYPE	Detached house
INTERNAL FLOOR AREA	163m²
NUMBER OF BEDROOMS	3
NUMBER OF PUBLIC ROOMS	2
PREDICTED ANNUAL HEATING COST	£333
SAP RATING	82 B
ENERGY USAGE (HEATING ONLY) IN kWh/m²	109 kWh/m²

FIGURE 1

FIGURE 2

FIGURE 3

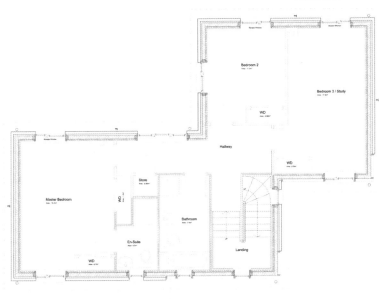

FIRST FLOOR

FIGURE 4

Historically, Highland house-types have been defined by an introverted nature, arising from the available materials and known construction systems, so reducing the possibilities of a direct relationship with the surrounding landscape. Utilising new and sustainable technologies, the Black House explores the potential of a spatial continuum between interior and exterior – minimising boundaries and drawing landscape and building together into one spatial discipline.

The house takes its name from the all over resin-based sprayed black coating, which references the traditional technique of tar-coating timber buildings.

KEY DESIGN FEATURES

A generous, open living space occupies the majority of the ground floor and offers a form of living in close proximity to the garden. The careful positioning of the kitchen island suggests the different areas of use within the room. In summer, the fully glazed facade can be opened up allowing it to connect directly with the garden.

The upper floor forms a sequence of cellular rooms, each of which is given its own character through the manipulation of the ceiling form and orientation.

At least one wall of each room incorporates a large glazed screen to heighten the relationship between inside and out.

CONSTRUCTION SYSTEM

The Black House utilises the properties of Multiplan cross laminated timber panels manufactured by Mayr-Melnhof Kaufmann in Austria. The panels are typically around 3m wide by up to 12.1m in length and in thicknesses of 140mm, 163mm and 220mm as required. The panels are exposed in the house interiors and were consequently specified with a visible furniture grade finish with service runs pre-routed into the panels in the factory. The timber structure is externally insulated and clad with fibre cement panels with a black resin-based spray applied waterproof finish to both walls and roof.

LESSONS LEARNED/KEY MESSAGES

The use of the cross laminated timber panel system has been successful with a minimum on site construction period for the structure, good quality robust, internal finish and has in-built sustainable credentials.

The ground level living space has a strong relationship with the garden and should work well with current modes of family living. We believe that the project demonstrates a sensible, economic approach to developing a low energy home, based on passive measures and a high performance envelope.

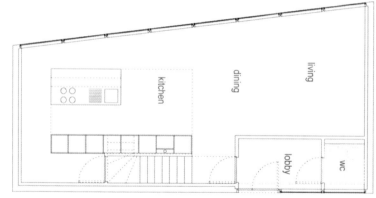

FIRST FLOOR

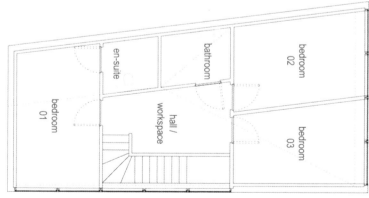

GROUND FLOOR

FIGURE 1

HOUSE NAME	Black House
ARCHITECT	Graeme Massie Architects
CONTRACTOR	O'Brien Homes
OWNER/ DEVELOPER	Highland Housing Alliance
HOUSE TYPE	Detached house
INTERNAL FLOOR AREA	116m²
NUMBER OF BEDROOMS	3
NUMBER OF PUBLIC ROOMS	1 (open plan ground floor)
PREDICTED ANNUAL HEATING COST	£138
SAP RATING	82
ENERGY USAGE (HEATING ONLY) IN kWh/m²	73 kWh/m²

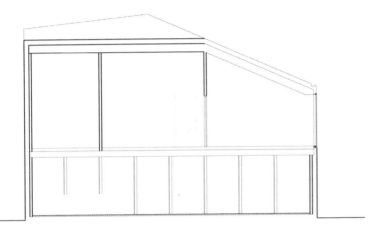

LONG SECTION

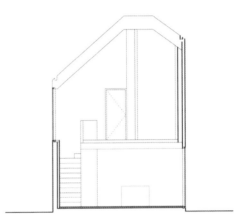

SHORT SECTION

FIGURE 2

22 HOUSE HS

From the outset the practice decided that we weren't interested in architectural grand-standing or designing houses with unnecessary expensive 'showy' architectural details. Instead we decided to consider, and to a degree accept, the limitations of the typical timber kit developer house. We wanted a well designed house that could then be easily built by a housing developer without a huge change in their methods and set-up. The initial feedback that we have had so far from contractors and fabricators seems to bear out the benefits of this.

The aim was to create a version of a suburban house type that did not have to rely on period details to feel homely, familiar or comfortable. The intention also seems to have been understood and appreciated by many of the visitors to the Expo.

KEY DESIGN FEATURES

The basic house type we developed, that all three of our houses are variations of, was designed to work as detached, semi-detached or even as a longer terrace.

On the Ground Floor we tried to remove as much circulation space as possible and to create simple plans that could accommodate a variety of different uses or scenarios (a young professional couple, a family, someone working from home, etc.) The layout of the ground floor is an attempt to create spaces that suggest rather than prescribe how they might be used. The upper hall was thought of as an additional room – perhaps a study or play space – rather than simply left over space used to access another room.

The houses are also designed to allow a degree of flexibility and even anticipate a degree of modification and internal alteration which could be made without resorting to major structural alterations – the double height void which was introduced to bring some south light into the north facing living room – this can be filled in to create an additional space on the first floor (one of the semi-detached houses has been built with this extra room included instead of the void).

CONSTRUCTION SYSTEM

The location in the North of Scotland did inform some of our material choices for the houses – we have used Scottish larch for much of the external cladding, and there is modesty and quietness in the design and in the robust detailing, that is appropriate to the location. We concentrated on designing a good external envelope using a natural building technology system – a highly insulated breathing construction.

LESSONS LEARNED/KEY MESSAGES

Looking around the site, it was very interesting and useful to see how others had approached the brief and tackled similar problems in different ways. On reflection, our houses like others on the site, could perhaps have benefited from being simpler in places. However the real test of the houses, and the most interesting part of the process, has yet to come with their inhabitation. Our houses have been designed to give the opportunity for a degree of internal alteration and modification – the simple structure means that internal walls can be added or removed and voids can be floored over. Externally, the cladding can be stained or painted – the garden can be cultivated. As with any typical suburban house it will be interesting to see how the new owners personalise and adjust the houses as they make them into their homes.

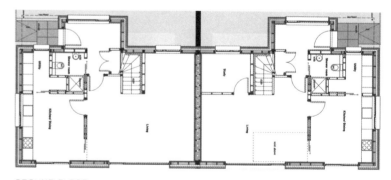

GROUND FLOOR

HOUSE NAME	HOUSE HS
ARCHITECT	Malcolm Fraser Architects
CONTRACTOR	Tulloch Homes Express
OWNER/ DEVELOPER	Highland Housing Alliance
HOUSE TYPE	2 Semi-detached houses
INTERNAL FLOOR AREA	House 1 – 109m²
	House 2 – 114m²
NUMBER OF BEDROOMS	3
NUMBER OF PUBLIC ROOMS	3
PREDICTED ANNUAL HEATING COST	£263
SAP RATING	82 B
ENERGY USAGE (HEATING ONLY) IN kWh/m²	114 kWh/m²

FIGURE 1

FIGURE 2

FIGURE 3

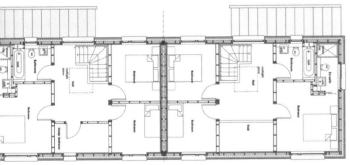

ST FLOOR

FIGURE 4

23 THE SKEWED HOUSE

One cannot use the word 'suburban' without triggering a slight prejudice amongst most architects. We approached the Expo, however, as an opportunity to explore a nascent idea about a rural housing cluster. This was partly a reaction to the maligned reputation of the suburban house but also a desire that the Expo's legacy should embrace more than a litany of individual house types.

We decided to challenge the competition masterplan and took the view that the Expo might be better served by a proposal for a larger cluster of houses as a more sustainable model for small remote settlements in the Highlands. Our initial competition entry, therefore, stretched over three neighbouring plots and reflected an ambition for a larger neighbourhood comprising six interconnecting courtyard houses. The 'Skewed House' embraces the benefits of courtyard living and offers an attractive mix of affordable, energy-efficient accommodation. Wrapped in cedar shingles, it avoids the monotonous, 'one-size-fits-all' approach which often generates anodyne, anonymous accommodation.

KEY DESIGN FEATURES

The scale of the internal rooms is deliberately modest in order to meet affordable benchmarks. Placing all of the rooms at ground level not only ensured that the houses are fully accessible, but also that the volume could be more easily stretched and modelled around the courtyard spaces.

Clustering houses together also allows you to form interesting, protected spaces between buildings. The composition of the buildings on the site inspired us to make an expressive alteration to the form of each house. We manipulated the conventional pitched roof by skewing the central ridge slightly so that it was no longer parallel with the eaves. This had the consequence of disrupting the repetitive nature of the interior spaces and generated some unexpected shifts in geometry. The short cross-sections reveal this variety but being an expressive gesture, we tested options by making a number of scale models, in order to make a considered judgment on the most suitable option.

CONSTRUCTION SYSTEM

The house design is single storey and comprises a heavily insulated timber frame structure, over-clad in cedar shingles.

We did not want the houses to be viewed as an assembly of planar walls supporting pitched roofs. Therefore the walls and roofs should visually merge together and timber shingles seemed well suited to that purpose. We realised that by adopting a timber frame and recycled insulation, we could build using entirely timber-based building products (with the exception of the internal plasterboard lining). Our aim was to provide an insulated and breathable building envelope to considerably more stringent U-value targets than the Building Standards.

LESSONS LEARNED/KEY MESSAGES

The Expo afforded us an opportunity to develop an affordable house type that could demonstrate an enduring connection to both the wider landscape and familiar rural typologies. However, we were disappointed that the Expo dropped its ambition to measure all the houses by one sustainable assessment methodology and failed to carry through a proposal for a bio-mass fuelled district heating system.

Despite these caveats, we were delighted to be invited to contribute to the Expo and consider 'The Skewed House' to be a successful and sustainable prototype of how to build for the future in rural Scotland.

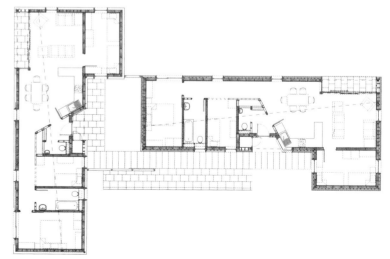

PLAN

HOUSE NAME	The Skewed House
ARCHITECT	Oliver Chapman Architects
CONTRACTOR	Tulloch Homes Express
OWNER/ DEVELOPER	Highland Housing Alliance
HOUSE TYPE	2 Detached houses
INTERNAL FLOOR AREA	Each house - 87m²
NUMBER OF BEDROOMS	3
NUMBER OF PUBLIC ROOMS	1
PREDICTED ANNUAL HEATING COST	£528
SAP RATING	
ENERGY USAGE (HEATING ONLY) IN kWh/m²	85 kWh/m²

FIGURE 1

FIGURE 2

FIGURE 3

FIGURE 4

FIGURE 5

PLOT

24 RED Homes

The concept for Responsive Environmental Design (RED) Homes is based on the idea of eco-minimalism. Sustainable design strategies have been blended with contemporary architecture by utilising ecological materials and solutions to minimise energy consumption.

The main aim was to develop a building with an adaptable plan and low energy consumption which avoids using 'tack-on' technologies such as photovoltaics and wind turbines. Large window openings were incorporated to provide high levels of day light and natural ventilation to help to enhance the quality of the internal environment. The building has been designed with a dark brick base course, a contrasting white render to the projecting lobby to highlight the entrance and provide a contrast to the timber cladding, all of which is softened by the larch cladding which will naturally weather to grey over time.

The building plot has been enhanced with a garden design by Hemingway Design.

KEY DESIGN FEATURES

The key design strategy was to minimise heat loss through the building envelope. This was achieved by using triple glazed timber frame windows and doors, high levels of thermal insulation (with U-values exceeding the minimum standards set in the Building Regulations) and ensuring while on site that the construction was as air tight as possible to minimise the building's air permeability. By minimising heat loss, the heating demand is reduced and therefore the associated carbon emissions are minimised.

Large well-insulated window openings optimise the use of natural daylight while reducing the requirement for artificial lighting without compromising energy efficiency. In addition the large openings optimise the buildings ability to cross ventilate, ensuring the internal environment has good air quality.

The insitu concrete ground floor slab with an integral underfloor heating system provides sufficient thermal mass to absorb warmth in the summer and release warmth in the winter.

CONSTRUCTION SYSTEM

A limited palette of low-maintenance high quality materials has been selected and where possible these have been locally sourced. The primary construction material is timber, with the external walls being manufactured off site to minimise on site construction times. The external walls are fully filled with 200mm locally sourced sheep's wool insulation.

The ground floor is an in-situ concrete slab with integral underfloor heating system. All windows and doors are triple glazed with timber frames and are clad with aluminium on the external face. Locally sourced untreated larch boards clad the external fabric.

LESSONS LEARNED/KEY MESSAGES

We believe Scotland's Housing Expo presented an opportunity to be part of a unique development with the potential to change the future of Scotland's housing.

In many cases the Expo was used as a test bed for sustainable design theory which we believe has resulted in a series of individual yet inspiring homes. Both positives and negatives can be taken from the design and construction process which will help refine Scotland's future housing designs.

We trust that the Expo will improve public awareness of the importance of sustainable design and will help stimulate the wider use of ecological materials and design strategies.

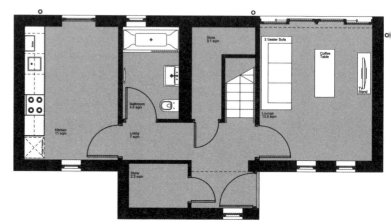

GROUND FLOOR

HOUSE NAME	RED Homes
ARCHITECT	McLean Architects
CONTRACTOR	Morrison Homes
OWNER/ DEVELOPER	Morrison Homes
HOUSE TYPE	2 Semi-detached houses
INTERNAL FLOOR AREA	Each house – 90m²
NUMBER OF BEDROOMS	2
NUMBER OF PUBLIC ROOMS	1
PREDICTED ANNUAL HEATING COST	£126
SAP RATING	85 B
ENERGY USAGE (HEATING ONLY) IN kWh/m²	101 kWh/m²

FIGURE 1

FIGURE 2

FIGURE 3

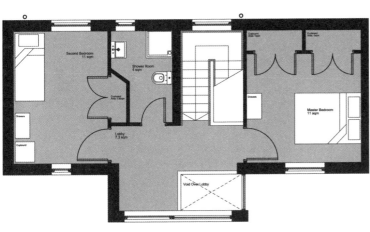

FIRST FLOOR

FIGURE 4

The competition design was for a 3-bedroom detached house with separate granny flat/live-work unit at the bottom of the garden. Entered through a double height sun-space located at the south west, the house is organised with living accommodation at first floor level and bedrooms and bathrooms located on the ground floor. A raised deck and covered drying area at first floor level provided a canopy to a bike store and parking spaces. Secondary entrances to the house were provided at ground floor level, directly adjacent to the car parking, and at the upper level, from the kitchen to the deck - providing a connection between living spaces and garden. Ultimately, the live-work unit, external stair, secondary entrances and first floor deck were omitted as cost savings.

KEY DESIGN FEATURES

The design of the Flower House tackles the issues of sustainability head-on but remains delightful and user friendly. Locating living spaces on the first floor gives the benefits of good day lighting from windows and rooflights and provides panoramic views to the Moray Firth. Bedrooms are situated on the ground floor but still take advantage of the south-east aspect. A storage wall and circulation form a buffer to the cold north-west side. The sun-space provides a bright and welcoming entrance, and creates a flexible extension to the living room on bright days or, the space can be closed off as a buffer to the outside. It also acts as a solar collector allowing the house to take advantage of the sun's energy.

CONSTRUCTION SYSTEM

The shell of the house is formed using Cross-Laminated timber (CLT) panels, fabricated to precise tolerances allowing it to be erected quickly and accurately with good air-tightness. Pavatherm wood-fibre insulation used for the walls and to the roof, has a laytex impregnated outer layer making it water resistant as well as breathable.

Horizontal timber boarding was designed to be turned at 72° to form the signature large daisy motifs. An extensive selection process to specify timber which could achieve the required durability, sustainability, fire resistance and price resulted in the use of biocide treated Scottish larch for the walls and fire retardant treated modified timber, Platowood for the roof both of which were sourced locally.

LESSONS LEARNED/KEY MESSAGES

The Flower House was designed to take full advantage of natural light and solar energy. Computer thermal modelling helped achieve an optimal balance between good levels of daylight and reduction in the need for artificial light, and solar gain without over-heating while limiting heat loss, thus resulting in a net benefit of useful energy to the building. Coupled with the use of prefabricated CLT, which offered effective airtightness, and good insulation, this resulted overall in a substantially reduced heating input requirement. Post occupancy evaluation would be required to provide the necessary data to fully assess the final building and performance.

Timber was selected as the main material for plot 25 due to its environmental credentials. The final building has timber cladding, wood fibre insulation and solid engineered timber panel external walls, roof and first floor. We were interested in using Cross Laminated Timber as this is a technology that has the potential to be produced in Scotland using the grade of timber that we grow in abundance.

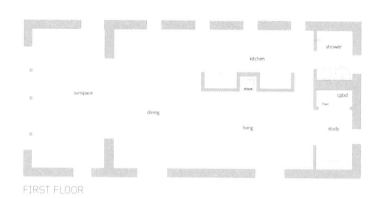

FIRST FLOOR

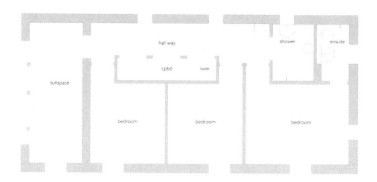

GROUND FLOOR

HOUSE NAME	The Flower House
ARCHITECT	A + J Burridge
CONTRACTOR	O'Brien Homes
OWNER/ DEVELOPER	Highland Housing Alliance
HOUSE TYPE	Detached house
INTERNAL FLOOR AREA	133m²
NUMBER OF BEDROOMS	3
NUMBER OF PUBLIC ROOMS	1
PREDICTED ANNUAL HEATING COST	£242
SAP RATING	C
ENERGY USAGE (HEATING ONLY) IN kWh/m²	123 kWh/m²

FIGURE 1

FIGURE 2

FIGURE 3

FIGURE 4

FIGURE 5

FIGURE 6

FIGURE 7

PLOT

26 THE HARDCORE SOFTHOUSE

The Hardcore Softhouse is a contemporary vernacular that considers the appropriate use of sustainable construction materials in a solar orientated design. Engineered to a BREEAM excellent rating in collaboration with the Buro Happold Sustainable and Alternative Technologies team, these highly efficient dwellings remain simple, intuitive and elegant pieces of rural architecture.

A strong, traditional, theme of heavy thermal core within a light insulating envelope underpins the design. Considered placement, orientation, fenestration and internal planning are supplemented by careful selections of materials and energy systems to achieve an un-conspicuously green result. The overall layout of buildings and landscape creates a sequence of internal and external landscapes aimed to support the day-to-day activities of family life.

KEY DESIGN FEATURES
The key generic component of each dwelling, which determined both its solar orientation and its relationship to the site and context as a whole, is a generous double height winter garden and circulation space. This is the primary point where the sun's light and energy enter the building. It is also the point where the public and private realms meet and overlap. Collectively it is the disposition of these elements that most influences the character of external space. Individually it elements most influences the spatial relationships, activities and delight within each house.

Closely related to the wintergarten is a central masonry core that both absorbs solar gain and houses all the building's secondary energy sources such as hot water, cooking and bathing. While in technical terms this moderates the internal environment, it is primarily seen as the psychological hearth and firmness of the home.

Surrounding the core area is a breathable envelope of lightweight construction, that serves to accommodate the more open plan, adaptable areas – the commodity of the dwelling which offers the requisite loose-fit for future patterns of use.

CONSTRUCTION SYSTEM
The entire production of construction materials and products and the labour required to assemble and maintain the dwellings was designed to draw on local Highland and other Scottish sources. The external envelope, a highly insulated breathable timber frame was manufactured in Elgin using locally sourced and recycled materials where possible. Durable, affordable and locally available, Scottish larch was chosen as the cladding finish, enhanced with a light stain to prolong its lifespan. The roof was clad in galvanised corrugated steel sheeting – now almost a vernacular element in the Scottish landscape and in itself recyclable.

Space heating and primary domestic hot water generation is provided by means of an externally sited air source heat pump system, connected to an indoor control station.

LESSONS LEARNED/KEY MESSAGES
Scottish rural architecture is traditionally characterised by a robust simplicity of form as displayed in the Hardcore Softhouse. We see this as an important progression as the growing emphasis on sustainability reinforces a need to return to more location-specific building in terms of siting, grouping, selection and source of materials and energy – a contemporary vernacular. At the same time, we believe that the careful placing of a fine piece of architecture – one which offers a firmness, commodity and delight – is the single most important step one can take towards sustainable development.

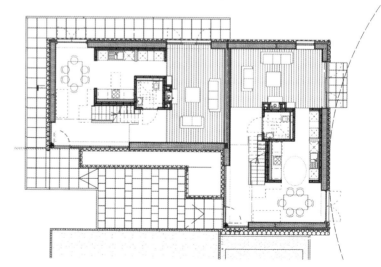

GROUND FLOOR

HOUSE NAME	The Hardcore Softhouse
ARCHITECT	Studio KAP Architects
CONTRACTOR	O'Brien Homes
OWNER/ DEVELOPER	Highland Housing Alliance
HOUSE TYPE	2 Semi-detached houses
INTERNAL FLOOR AREA	Each House – 113m²
NUMBER OF BEDROOMS	3
NUMBER OF PUBLIC ROOMS	2
PREDICTED ANNUAL HEATING COST	£260
SAP RATING	83 B
ENERGY USAGE (HEATING ONLY) IN kWh/m²	106 kWh/m²

FIGURE 1

FIGURE 2

FIGURE 3

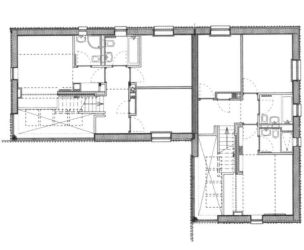

FIRST FLOOR

FIGURE 4

FIGURE 5

27 HOUSE NS

From the outset the practice decided that we weren't interested in architectural grand-standing or designing houses with unnecessary expensive "showy" architectural details. Instead we decided to consider, and to a degree accept, the limitations of the typical timber kit developer house. We wanted a well designed house that could then be easily built by a housing developer without a huge change in their methods and set-up. The initial feedback that we have had so far from contractors and fabricators seems to bear out the benefits of this.

The aim was to create a version of a suburban house type that did not have to rely on period details to feel homely, familiar or comfortable. The intention also seems to have been understood and appreciated by many of the visitors to the Expo.

KEY DESIGN FEATURES

The basic house type we developed, that all three of our houses are variations of, was designed to work as detached, semi-detached or even as a longer terrace.

On the Ground Floor we tried to remove as much circulation space as possible and to create simple plans that could accommodate a variety of different uses or scenarios (a young professional couple, a family, someone working from home, etc.) The layout of the ground floor is an attempt to create spaces that suggest rather than prescribe how they might be used. The upper hall was thought of as an additional room – perhaps a study or play space – rather than simply left over space used to access another room.

The houses are also designed to allow a degree of flexibility and even anticipate a degree of modification and internal alteration which could be made without resorting to major structural alterations – the double height void which was introduced to bring some south light into the north facing living room – this can be filled in to create an additional space on the first floor (one of the neighbouring semi-detached houses has been built with this extra room included instead of the void).

CONSTRUCTION SYSTEM

The location in the North of Scotland did inform some of our material choices for the houses – we have used Scottish larch for much of the external cladding, and there is perhaps a modesty and quietness in the design and in the robust detailing, that is appropriate to the location. We concentrated on designing a good external envelope using a natural building technology system – a highly insulated breathing construction.

LESSONS LEARNED/KEY MESSAGES

As with any project you learn a lot! Looking around the site it was very interesting and useful to see how others had approached the brief and tackled similar problems in different ways. On reflection, our houses like others on the site, could perhaps have benefited from being simpler in places.

However the real test of the houses, and the most interesting part of the process, has yet to come with their inhabitation. Our houses have been designed to give the opportunity for a degree of internal alteration and modification – the simple structure means that internal walls can be added or removed and voids can be floored over. Externally, the cladding can be stained or painted – the garden can be cultivated. As with any typical suburban house it will be interesting to see how the new owners personalise and adjust the houses as they make them into their homes.

HOUSE NAME	House NS
ARCHITECT	Malcolm Fraser Architects
CONTRACTOR	Tulloch Homes Express
OWNER/ DEVELOPER	Highland Housing Alliance
HOUSE TYPE	Detached house
INTERNAL FLOOR AREA	109m²
NUMBER OF BEDROOMS	3
NUMBER OF PUBLIC ROOMS	2
PREDICTED ANNUAL HEATING COST	£274
SAP RATING	83 B
ENERGY USAGE (HEATING ONLY) IN kWh/m²	114 kWh/m²

FIGURE 1

FIGURE 2

FIGURE 3

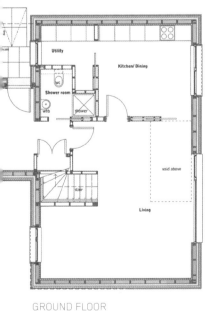

GROUND FLOOR

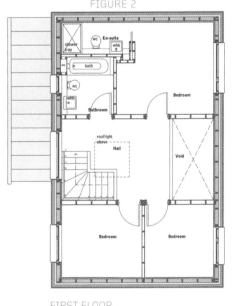

FIRST FLOOR

FIGURE 4

FIGURE 6.16

THE PLAY AREA
PARKS AND PLACES

The Play Area provides play space for children from 2 to 12 years. It forms part of a network of attractive routes, pocket parks, streets corners and meeting places across the site that allow outdoor living, play and an active lifestyle.

Cadell² with Timberplay

Cadell², masterplanners for the Expo site, along with Timberplay, a specialist supplier of play equipment, have worked together to design a playground for the Expo site that responds to the local landscape and topography.

Key facts about the Play Area

Design. The Play Area is designed as a miniature landscape including its own hillside, trees, village, beach and wildlife. The use and expression of larch in the construction of the play equipment allows hands-on contact with trees trunks, tree-houses and timber sculpture.

Construction. Ground-modelling, planting and a simple palette of natural materials establish a visual calm that is consistent with the design of the streets.

Equipment

Small Play House. Small see-saw. Snail. Climbing Structure. Quadro Hammock Seat. Wobble Dish. Construction Site with Slide.

⊙sust.

AFTER THE EVENT

CHAPTER 7

" The true effectiveness of delivery of
the masterplan objectives can be seen
in the interaction between the elements
of completed architecture and public
realm."

FIGURE 71

FIGURE 72

FIGURE 73

" Walking routes are integrated with housing throughout the site. The use of Caithness stone signals the 'pedestrian only' routes linking the extensive framework of shared surfaces."

FIGURE 74

WERE THE AIMS OF THE MASTERPLAN REALISED?

In the view of the masterplanner, the Urban Design Objectives of the masterplan have been largely realised in the Expo. Some elements of the planned public realm and architecture were missing, or were omitted in the run-up to the August 2010 event because of time and budget constraints. These included: delayed and incomplete houses and home office units; missing garden boundaries, paving materials, re-cycling stations and street furniture; and missing trees at the top of the Avenue. The majority of these elements were due to timing and logistics difficulties, but they were completed after the public event. The built architecture also reflects some significant design development since the winning competition entries. Whilst in many cases this has led to a positive distillation of ideas there were also some disappointing losses.

The true effectiveness of delivery of the masterplan objectives can be seen in the interaction between the elements of completed architecture and public realm. To capture this interaction, some of the successes and failures of the interplay between architecture, public realm and masterplan are reviewed in the captions to the following photographs, taken during the Expo event [Figures 7.1 to 7.17].

7.1 This bridge, a key orientation point on the site, was the designed gateway into the site during the Expo event.

7.2 NORD's Plot 2 best represents the masterplan aim of a simple and imaginative re-invention of an indigenous form: the rural terrace.

7.3 Walking routes are integrated with housing throughout the site. The use of Caithness stone signals the 'pedestrian only' routes linking the extensive framework of shared surfaces.

7.4 Robust and urban: Whilst JM Architects Plot 1 terrace is not masonry as planned, the use of ivy-clad green walls gives an intriguing prospect of the architecture being absorbed as landscape over time.

"The main success was the delivery of the majority of the wealth of ambition reflected in the competition architecture and earlier in the masterplan and stakeholders expectations"

7.5 The Mews [seen with incomplete paving] re-invents the Scottish Close as a service space for adjoining houses. The location of a series of detached office and studio units that can share facilities, this is planned for 21st century working from home.

7.6 One of a row of three dual-fronted plots with a frontage and front door to the Green and a separate office entrance to the Close.

7.7 This view captures the material qualities of masonry in the foreground elevation and in the paving of reclaimed setts set against the transition to timber-clad houses and distant landscape. The Green is unenclosed due to the lack of three terraced houses intended at the north edge.

7.8 The house-fronts to the Green demonstrate the intended variations within architecture by three separate practices whilst frontages and scale are consistent. Deeply modelled elevations boldly interact with the street and the main public space.

FIGURE 7.5

FIGURE 7.6

FIGURE 7.7

FIGURE 7.8

FIGURE 7.9

7.9 The turf wall. Some of the planned street furniture was completed, helping to link ideas of materiality and landform with informal places to rest and for children to play.

7.10 Distinctive architecture, with the urban-scaled gesture of a 2-storey window, helps anchor the principal public space on the site.

FIGURE 7.10

FIGURE 7.11

7.11 This is the distant view of the Moray Firth and Ben Wyvis around which the Green and Brae were designed. The street and this view will be better framed, as intended, when the missing Plot 10 houses are constructed.

7.12 Incomplete boundaries, a missing studio building, and a house smaller than planned, all contribute to an unplanned gap in the street frontage to the Avenue.

FIGURE 7.12

7.13 The landscape structure is successfully drawn into the site, entrances reached by bridging across the surface-water swale. These elements combine with the timber-clad houses at the eastern edge of the site to create a strong forest-edge character.

7.14 This opening in the street leads to one of the walking routes into the countryside. The gable windows of the Malcolm Fraser designed houses help this route feel safe and welcoming.

7.15 Brennan and Wilson's Plot 18 house responds well to the street corner and the changing characteristics of different street types.

7.16 This view up the Avenue shows the route as part street and part landscape, the swale signifying the break.

7.17 The play space is a very visible, un-segregated and lively part of the street.

FIGURE 7.13

FIGURE 7.14

FIGURE 7.15

FIGURE 7.17

FIGURE 7.16

HOW COULD THE COMPETITION SELECTION PROCESS AND THE DELIVERY OF THE HOUSING BE IMPROVED?

A THEME

The main success was the delivery of the majority of the wealth of ambition reflected in the competition architecture and earlier in the masterplan and stakeholders expectations. It could be argued that this original ambition over-reached the capacity of the project or the economic circumstances to fully support or deliver it, leading to a number of procurement set-backs. Had it not been for the recession, the housing might have been completed earlier, however the likelihood is that many of the same problems would still have arisen as the original funding model was too complex. The ambition was very great indeed with many architects aspiring to the best European and Scandinavian standards of detail quality and energy performance, where often the culture and practices of building industries are a world apart. This is linked to several aspects of the project that could have been handled differently.

A weakness of a first Housing Fair or Expo was always likely to be the attempt to do everything at once, taking on multiple aspirations, from multiple perspectives and to try to get it all right first time. In addition, perhaps the Expo Board was trying too hard to emulate the Finns.

The aims of stakeholders were all valid, but collectively were perhaps too dilute. The housing, as built, reflects the diversity of agendas quite well, with good examples in most categories, but the lessons learned and future gains are less discernible than they might have been. There was not a single overarching theme as a focus for the ambition. Reaching consensus on such a theme would have helped the project and may only have taken a month of exploring and discussing options in 2006.

In the view of the masterplanner the Expo could have been successful as an event with any one of the following as a primary theme:
- timber construction
- prototype volume housing
- energy-efficient housing
- 21st century living
- regional architecture – a new vernacular
- localism
- placemaking.

FIGURE 7.18

PLOT SIZE

The plots were limited to a maximum of four houses [the terraces at Plots 1 and 2] or six flats [Plot 8]. Most were single houses [14 out of 27 plots]. The rest were semi-detached, pairs or 3-house terraces. The difficulties of financing 27 divergent individual plot types, with the intermixture of private and affordable tenures, had an impact throughout the delivery of the housing. This affected the individual deliverability of every private house plot, where delivery was dependant on the involvement of private sector developers and contractors, and where commercial clients were needed with both the capacity to employ architects and signed-up to the architectural ideas from the start. The recession of 2008 led to a funding crisis for the Expo and the resultant need to change the approach to delivery by moving to a design and build approach. Notwithstanding this it might have been easier to manage such an event in future with a reduced number of plots and a larger number of similar house types – even in better economic circumstances.

Fewer larger plots would have a number of advantages:
- economics of bulk procurement and standardisation
- greater coherence
- more consistent quality of construction
- fewer, more committed, designers
- fewer boundaries and interfaces between designers (and developers)
- reduced infrastructure costs
- reduced project management costs.

However, fewer larger plots would have reduced the 'wow factor', as there would have been less opportunity for a wide variety of house designs. One of the elements most liked by the visiting public was the number of different house types on show. So this would also have to be taken into consideration, depending on the scale of a future Expo.

COMMUNICATIONS

More time allocated to direct communication between masterplanner, infrastructure designers and plot designers would have helped enormously and this would have benefited from full endorsement at management level from the outset. This came later in the project but it was needed from the start. This issue was raised at post-event meetings by a number of architects, many of whom expressed disappointment at the lack of opportunity to work in collaboration with those on adjacent plots or using similar materials, which could have helped streamline procurement and logistical delivery issues.

FIGURE 7.19

FIGURE 7.20

FIGURE 7.21

On moving to the design and build model, there was a degree of breakdown in communication between the architects and the developers, particularly during the value engineering exercise. This could have been eased by encouraging a more collaborative approach from the outset, but by this point, time was in short supply.

In addition, although the six contractors who delivered the houses and infrastructure, reported that they really enjoyed the opportunity to work collaboratively on site (which they felt worked extremely successfully), oddly, one architect who delivered houses on two plots had worked with a different contractor on each.

An 'Extranet' was set up to facilitate dialogue between the architects. This was reported to have had some value as a commonly accessible database, for design information in particular. It held a large number of drawings of the infrastructure and plots but it was an inadequate substitute for direct discussion, understanding of other agendas and resolution of design interfaces in person.

However, many architects underused it, leading to discrepancies between the later detailed plot layouts and infrastructure design that had been detailed much earlier. Although several co-ordination meetings were arranged between infrastructure and plot teams in 2008 and 2009, these were under-attended by architects struggling without clients or appointments. The meetings were difficult to arrange and often quite superficial due to time constraints. If another event such as this is considered, sufficient time and resources need to be allocated to such key meetings.

Whilst the masterplanners helped Highland Housing Alliance to monitor the post-competition design changes by remote email reviewing of the submissions made, due to time and other pressures, some architects did not participate fully in keeping these records flowing, and so this work was incomplete. Thus, although a degree of design co-ordination and monitoring did occur, this was against a general background of limited resources, and is another issue that would have to be addressed in any future Expo.

FIGURE 7.22

FIGURE 7.23

FIGURE 7.24

FIGURE 7.25

PRIVATE SECTOR DEVELOPERS ROLE

Architects were asked to involve developers from the outset, however this was not mandatory. Whilst this point may be academic, since many of those architects who had development partners lost them as a result of the economic downturn, the fact that many architects had no client for much of the project had a significant impact. A commercial critic would have been helpful from the outset for all projects, as well as making sure that the contractor/developer organisations used were robust enough to be capable of investing in architects and design team fees up-front. As it turned out, the project went forward with six such developer/contractors.

It was suggested that in other places and for a future Expo the organisers should consider using one or more of the several specialised private sector developers in existence who are familiar with design-led procurement processes, and who would be capable of stepping up to act as lead(s) for the procurement of infrastructure and to meet the broader agenda of a national design event such as the Expo. These conditions are not uncommon in the cities and on sites with high historical or urban sensitivity.

PROJECT MANAGEMENT

Value engineering, a painful process for designers and client who have expended time and resources on detailed design, might have been obviated by co-ordinated cost planning at RIBA stages C (Outline Proposals) and D (Detailed Proposals) (Ref 7.1). However, some of the innovations that were originally planned were adversely affected by the economic downturn internationally.

For example, when an early proposal to produce mass timber components in Scotland from Scottish timber, supported by local companies and the Forestry Commission Scotland became economically unviable due to the lack of a supply chain locally. This resulted in a frenzy of activity to secure mass timber components from elsewhere in Europe at prices that had immediately increased due to the decline of the Pound against the Euro. This point is made to reinforce that fact that some issues related to value engineering were forced by events beyond the control of the designers, developers and Expo organisers and these might not have arisen in more stable economic times. This is one of a number of examples, including the lack of suitably certified, locally available materials and components, which again were adversely affected by rises in prices in other parts of Europe. There is a need to develop local markets and supply chains in order to buffer the effect of such external factors.

There is also a clear need to take account of all external risks when preparing programmes and economic models for any such event.

FIGURE 7.26

FIGURE 7.27

A linked design and project management agenda and methodology, with clearer mutually established definitions of professional responsibilities, would also have helped the infrastructure and event management processes enormously. These issues are discussed further in Chapter 8.

FEEDBACK FROM THE EVENT

The key objective of the Expo was to showcase innovative, sustainable housing and placemaking to a wide audience to help change attitudes towards house and place design. Since the event, a number of studies and reviews have commenced with a view to collecting both anecdotal and formal feedback on the impact that the event has had in this respect. Research is still ongoing, and the outcomes and recommendations are not available at the time of writing.

The following was recorded officially through visitor surveys (although there were also informal visits by various other organisations):
- visitor numbers over the month exceeded the target of 30,000 by more than 10%;
- the event attracted visitors from at least 28 of Scotland's Council areas;

- advanced ticket purchase from other parts of the UK included places as far away as: Brighton, Essex, Bristol, North Wales and Northern Ireland;
- visitors from other countries included Australia, France, Finland, the Republic of Ireland, Norway and the USA;
- school groups and college students visited from: Inverness, Plockton, Aboyne, Ullapool, Bettyhill and Inverness College;
- housing associations from Skye, Lochaber, Edinburgh, Perthshire, Glasgow, Argyll and Aberdeen;
- council visits from Dundee, Edinburgh, Shetland, Western Isles, East Lothian, North Lanarkshire, Moray, Aberdeenshire, Dumfries & Galloway, Glasgow;
- visits by a number of professional bodies including the RIAS, RTPI, Homes for Scotland, the Scottish Construction Forum, SHON (the Scottish HECA Officers Network), Scottish Ecological Design Association, the Forest Industry Advisory Board, the Timber Development Programme, etc.;
- visits by Scotland's First Minister, and several other Scottish Government Ministers, leaders of the opposition parties, MSPs, MEPs, MPs and senior civil servants.

VISITOR FEEDBACK

The following section summarises the general feedback from visitors and the house ambassadors:

- more than 80% of visitors who responded to the Expo feedback questionnaire said that the Expo met or exceeded their expectations, more than 60% said it exceeded them;
- over 78% of respondents said their visit to the Expo had given them ideas about the type of house they might live in in future or internal or external features they might consider for their current or future house;
- over 77% of respondents would consider attending a future Expo;
- over 42% of respondents were keen to attend a future Expo;
- over 77% of respondents who said they might attend a future Expo would be prepared to travel up to 200 miles to visit it.

The following feedback was gathered from organisations and business representatives from a separate survey by The Highland Council and through post event focus groups:

- the competition gave architects across the country a much needed opportunity to get involved in an innovative enterprise – too few competitions of this type exist;
- the role of the masterplan in pulling the development together cohesively, was widely appreciated;
- professional visitors and the wider public were challenged and stimulated by the Expo;
- visitors reported that the Expo was a great way of getting people talking about what we mean by housing and community;
- the housebuilders found the public to be generally receptive to new ideas and the Expo showed that good architecture is not inaccessible;

FIGURE 7.28

- people felt that added value was triggered by the seminars and other events, which provided opportunities to meet people from a broad range of interests and learn from different disciplines;
- similarly, the activities provided for children, from the collecting of 'trump'-style cards with individual house details, to pond dipping, the play area and 'Claystation' (which provided an opportunity to build your own Expo house and locate it on a plot of your choosing) not only engaged with the house-buyer of the future, but also appealed to the adult population;
- overall, the event had a positive impact on planning officers, housebuilders and building-designers;
- it provided an opportunity for collaboration across the built environment professions, including shared skills learning;
- it provided opportunities for small and medium sized companies to try out new ideas, from innovative design solutions to skills development;
- the Expo also provided an opportunity for the public and professionals to mix in the same forum, especially through the seminars – but it was suggested that these could have been better advertised as public events;
- there was general agreement that there should be more Expos to build on what was achieved by this first experiment under difficult economic conditions and extreme weather during the construction period.

The following feedback was gathered from the wider visiting public:
- the scale and diversity of the Expo provided a definite 'wow factor';
- visitors were impressed by the innovative features in some of the houses and appreciated the levels to which some of the house ambassadors had researched the associated technologies and building fabric aspects of the houses they were responsible for;
- the biggest attraction from a public point of view was the variety and openness of the site – seldom do the public get such an opportunity to see so much in one place;
- the provision for children was excellent, which was particularly important given the long average stay by visiting groups;
- general interest was expressed in buying the houses when they are ready for sale;
- the events on sustainability themes were welcomed and appreciated in terms of raising the level of debate and understanding on these issues for the wider public;
- visitors were given ideas that were applicable to their own houses or self-build aspirations including the demonstration of low cost energy solutions;
- the role of the Expo in supporting the construction sector and apprenticeships during a downturn was highlighted as a huge positive.

Furthermore, it was reported that the event provides a legacy of 52 quite 'different' houses at Milton of Leys, an area earmarked for expansion, including 20 affordable homes. This in itself provides a useful forum for debate for those members of the public and professionals with a desire to innovate.

It was felt that there were key aspects that could have been improved. These included:
- the event was poorly marketed nationally beyond the Highlands;
- the completion of more of the houses, internally and externally, although this was a contentious issue, as professionals and the public in many cases appreciated the value of work in progress and the opportunity to see construction make-up. It was even argued by some that there should be more unfinished examples but that they should be exploited for educational purposes;
- the landscaping and gardens were incomplete, it would have given a better impression of what the place will be like to live in if a degree of maturity in planting had been achieved;
- there was a lack of availability of specialists on site to answer questions about housing design, key features and energy systems and usage;
- there was a lack of technical information generally;
- the scale of opportunities to spend money on the site both through the lack of a trade village and the catering provision could have been expanded to provide a better experience for the high visitor numbers and to generate more revenue;
- more progress before the harsh winter of 2009/10, might have encouraged keener participation in equipping and furnishing the houses (other than those discussed in Chapter 5) and in providing ancillary services to visitors on-site – this must be addressed in any future event;
- the car parking area was inadequate – too small and poorly finished;
- on- and off-site signage was inadequate, particularly from the main routes to the site from Inverness and the south;
- earlier house valuations could have helped promote sales, but are also of general interest to the public and professionals alike;
- wheelchair access and accessibility generally within some of the houses and around the site could have been better;
- one objective was to promote more use of locally sourced timber, and other Scottish components and materials, this was inadequately exploited.

One point raised in relation to the success or otherwise of such an event is the need for a true champion to promote it.

The following chapter explores in greater detail some of the points raised above and the impact of the delivery process on the final outcomes, highlighted through the architects' experiences.

Johnny Cadell, Cadell2 LLP
The Highland Council
Lori McElroy

ACHIEVEMENTS AND LESSONS FOR THE FUTURE

CHAPTER 8

" Scotland's first Housing Expo aspires
to be a catalyst for the country's
building industry, by creating an
exemplar community which will act
as an inspiration for future housing
design and development"

FIGURE 8.1

CONCEPT TO REALITY

As suggested in previous chapters, there was no agreed process that the originators of the concept of Scotland's (first) Housing Expo could refer to or develop from. It was possible to draw upon the Finnish model, but knowledge there had evolved over forty years, and it was not possible to absorb and take advantage of all of this expertise. In order to deliver an Expo in Scotland, collectively the teams had to take the plunge and trust in one another. Some things were lost along the way, some innovations survived the journey and new ideas emerged: in some cases to the detriment of original ideas and in others by improving the initial proposals. There also emerged situations where the experience of what the Expo achieved is being adapted for incorporation on future projects.

As might be expected, each of the architects approached the brief differently, with a vast range of materials and techniques used to demonstrate an approach to sustainable design. This chapter takes an in-depth look at the experiences and lessons learned on a variety of the Expo projects where the architects faced particular challenges. These highlight the considerable effort required in retaining and testing new ideas under the design and build procurement model, compared with the originally envisaged traditional architect/contractor approach.

The chapter also explores some of the lessons learned and makes comment on issues to consider should another Expo take place in Scotland, based on the first hand experiences of those involved this time around.

SURVIVAL OF THE FITTEST?

Scotland's first Housing Expo aspired to be a catalyst for the country's building industry, by creating an exemplar community which will act as an inspiration for future housing design and development.

Key objectives were to:
- showcase creative design solutions to encourage an improvement in design standards in public and private sector housing;
- create a sustainable living environment with a focus on the use of local materials and low energy houses;
- encourage technological and construction innovation;
- encourage a step change within sectors of the building industry including component suppliers and self-builders;
- capture public imagination and raise expectations in house design;
- promote a distinctive local vernacular;
- promote the creativity and quality of lifestyle of the Highlands to residents and visitors;
- exploit regional development opportunities including trade links and local manufacturing potential;
- encourage innovation in interior and product design;
- enable future Expos to act as a catalyst in assisting in the regeneration of smaller communities.

The extent to which these were achieved is discussed below.

PROCUREMENT ROUTE

Post competition, it became apparent that some of the architects did not yet have developers in place, and the emerging economic difficulties in 2008 threatened to jeopardise the delivery of the project. This prompted a decision to delay the event from August 2009 to August 2010. The decision was also taken at that time to re-brand the event as Scotland's Housing Expo (rather than the Highland Housing Fair). As 2008 rolled on, with many of the original developers unable to secure the finance required to take individual projects forward, the economic climate forced the client body to rethink their procurement strategy. Early in 2009, the Board (on the advice of a number of sources) agreed that if there was to be any chance of delivering an Expo in August 2010, the procurement route would have to be changed. It was concluded that while the model of delivering 27 plots with 27 architect/contractor/developer teams works in Finland, this approach was one that would be difficult to implement in Scotland under the Construction (Design and Management) Regulations. And while it might have been possible to resolve this, it would be difficult to do so within the required timescales.

Without such a hugely committed client body and a determined Expo Board, not to mention the hard work of all involved, this was a project which might not have made it to the opening day. The Expo came to fruition because the organisations listed in Reference 1.2, bought-in to a vision with no guarantees and held their nerve.

FIGURE 8.2

The necessary funding was eventually secured and with increasing pressure to deliver the Expo within budget, a revised procurement strategy was devised. With the benefit of hindsight, there were consequences which could not have been fully anticipated when the decision was made to fix a date of August 2010 and to change from a traditional contract approach to design and build. At the time, in terms of delivering cost certainty and driving best-value, this was perhaps the only viable route for the client body. But many of the architects involved were not used to working with developers in this way and had expected a greater degree of input to detail design and construction on site. Their priority was to deliver their winning competition entries and to meet all of the competition objectives they had signed up to when selected. The developers on the other hand were used to a procurement process where they were firmly in control of delivery – their commitment was to deliver on time, and to a budget, which had to take precedence over the competition objectives.

With the exception of the few situations where there was an existing developer/architect relationship, the new delivery model created new design/construction teams which took some time to build trust and understanding. Specifically, the architects were conscious of the need to balance cost control and best value against the Expo's aspiration for a high quality, exemplary finished product.

The new delivery process was not helped by the design competition, which being an open competition, had not required designs to be taken to a level where detailed cost information could be provided. The competition had a technical panel to advise on issues such as buildability, sustainability and cost; and the judging panel made the selection of winners on the basis of this advice and other factors including design and fit with the masterplan/ design framework. As has been explained in Chapter 3, changes to the masterplan were necessary to accommodate the judges' selection of projects for a variety of reasons.

Some plots were very popular – with a number of excellent entries, while others had no entries at all. Some of the required changes were to be expected and could be easily accommodated, but for some of the winners, the knock-on effect had very significant consequences. This was particularly the case where a house designed for a 'private' plot was allocated an affordable housing site, with all the cost restrictions that follow. The architects were then required to re-design the houses as affordable homes, reducing floor areas and budgets to prescribed benchmarks for no additional fee. While costs were initially less of an issue in the privately funded designs, the impact of the banking crisis made it impossible to secure funding and valuations began to fall. The issue of the inequity between 'price' and 'value' became clear when the positive benefits of capital investment made to reduce life-cycle cost was not taken into account in the valuation of a property.

To illustrate the impacts of the challenges experienced in delivery, a number of examples of the impacts of decisions made at the judging stage, as a consequence of the changes to the procurement process and the financial climate are outlined below. These are followed by some significant examples that made it all the way through the process and which are now beginning to have a positive impact on house construction in Scotland.

FIGURE 8.3

VALUE ENGINEERING

Early involvement from the constructors focused mainly on construction advice and cost control, but as the projects developed many of the projects had to be value engineered in conjunction with the contractors to ensure that they could be built more cost effectively. This made the project development process more challenging for all involved. The experience was more constructive for some than for others, much depended on the amount of time that each practice could set aside for dialogue during an unprecedented economic downturn, and a severe winter that made travel around Scotland extremely challenging.

Throughout this process the architects and design teams all battled hard to maintain their original competition winning concepts, some of which were more robust than others. To succeed, they had to not only stick passionately to their concepts, but to work hard alongside the client and contractor to adapt and evolve their schemes with integrity and conviction. The impact of the change in contract type is discussed generally below, and more specifically in the case studies in Chapter 6.

" The project architects were asked to highlight the signature element of their building, with a view to establishing what was and what was not negotiable. This resulted in changes in some projects for a variety of reasons."

The outcomes extended beyond the common understanding of 'success' or 'failure'. While positive engagement and an acceptance of the cost constraints worked to the advantage of some projects, for others solutions that met the needs of both designer and contractor were more difficult to achieve. It was not a matter of resistance or submission to the process, the most successful projects in some cases were achieved through intense collaboration, but others were simply easier to resolve. Similarly, for some, solutions seemed forever beyond reach, despite engagement between teams. Every project was different.

FIGURE 8.4

The project architects were asked to highlight the signature element of their building, with a view to establishing what was and what was not negotiable. This resulted in material changes in some projects and for the majority the removal of features such as solar thermal and rainwater harvesting tanks, for financial and other reasons. These could all have been considered supplementary to a building that is inherently sustainable due to its energy efficiency and material use, and many of the architects reported subsequently that the removal of these systems had little or no impact on performance. However, the expected future changes to Building Standards will strongly encourage the inclusion of renewables at one level or other. This raises a potential dilemma for the future and the need to decide our priorities for investment: should this be in fabric and passive measures or in renewables?

At the end of the day the challenge remained constant: to push the boundaries of housing design and low energy sustainable strategies, to create an Expo site that was about raising the bar for Scottish and UK housing and in the longer term to encourage a step change in the industry.

INNOVATION MUST BE FOLLOWED THROUGH

To the credit of those who designed the houses and those who delivered the Expo, there was a clear desire to ensure that the architectural appearances of the designs remained true to the competition winning entries as far as possible. But appearances can be deceiving in some cases, and beauty is (sometimes) only skin deep.

" At the end of the day the challenge remained constant: to push the boundaries of housing design and low energy sustainable strategies, to create an Expo site that was about raising the bar and in the longer term to encourage a step change in the industry."

A number of the winning designs adopted innovative construction systems, some of which were critical to the performance of the dwelling. Decisions to modify construction systems need to take full account of the consequences for environmental performance. A few examples are discussed below.

The replacement of a dark coloured masonry wall, which is designed to act as a solar energy store in a Trombe-Michel (Ref 8.1) wall construction, has a greater impact than making a cost saving for example — it totally disrupts the thermal performance of the dwelling and results in the need for an alternative approach to maintaining a comfortable internal thermal environment. In attempting to address the challenges of climate change, the low carbon economy and the associated demands of increasingly stringent Building Standards, we have to begin to understand that as buildings are evolving, the fabric is becoming part of, and in some instances is replacing, conventional energy systems. Value engineering also has to evolve by dealing with the 'whole' and not the sum of the parts.

In another project, a highly insulated, air-tight massive timber design, the architect was frustrated by specific savings which seemed to go counter to the specification. This timber house was very airtight, but because of a requirement for cost savings, the air-source heat pump and ventilation system were deleted. This could have negative implications for the resultant air quality, and condensation risk, as a forced system is normally required for air quality control in such an airtight building, despite this being a breathing construction.

On another Plot, on visiting the site during the construction the architect observed that temporary weather protection to the timber panels was poor, resulting in 'capping' (expansion at the edges of the timber units due to moisture absorption) of some of the finished surfaces. This demonstrates that even in cases where the original concepts survived intact, a lack of understanding of the materials or construction system in some cases compromised the end result.

Generally, there was concern expressed at the quality of some of the workmanship, particularly the fixing of insulation and air-tightness.

The issue of non-negotiables in buildings where the fabric is a determinant of performance is not new, or one confined to the Expo project. But it is essential, as we move forward with new ideas to address climate change mitigation and diminishing fossil fuel reserves, that all members of the design and construction industry re-skill in order to appreciate the potential impacts of what seem on the face of it to be logical decisions.

FIGURE 8.5

FIGURE 8.6

THE DEVIL IS IN THE DETAIL

After novation to the 5 contractors, some of the architects reported that value engineering commenced immediately. Even those who felt that they had costs tied down were advised that in the interests of time and the tight delivery schedule, some of the construction innovations would have to be simplified. There was no suggestion that the house layouts should be changed, and while the contractors argued that the impact would be minimal as the volumes and spaces created would not be affected by materials changes, as already highlighted, for some of the designs, materials were an integral part of the design proposal.

Retention of the key elements of the landscape design was a key factor in delivering the objectives of the masterplan. This presented challenges for all the teams within the tight budget and time-pressured delivery schedule. For example, an obvious saving for the contractors might have been the boundary walls around the Terrace and the Close. However, for the masterplanner this element was critical to address the Avenue and animate the Green. Recognising this, the architects with plots located in this vicinity argued to retain these elements and despite some material changes, the fundamental elements were delivered.

In a few cases, external finishes were lost and material quality was reduced. In some situations the architects felt that they could accommodate the requested changes as these were not the key feature of their houses, in others the sacrifices were more difficult to accommodate.

With the full support of the delivery team, one project architect worked especially hard to retain the design's signature stone walls. Another gave up a similar feature for other gains. The former project was just completed in time for the event, but retention of the external finish meant that compromises were made in the quality of the interior finishes, fixtures and fittings, and internal layout to remain within budget.

One affordable house project reduced the quality of the massive timber kit used to ensure delivery, while others, convinced that their projects could be built on time and within budget, stuck to the original plan. The components for the massive timber private dwellings were delivered, but in some cases, too late for completion in time for the event. Another, originally designed as housing for sale, was re-allocated to an affordable housing plot and remains un-built.

In summary, lack of direct control over delivery, due to the design and build process, meant that the innovative construction approach was in the hands of the contractor, rather than the architect who was in most cases working without support of the occupier- client.

SETTING TARGETS/MONITORING AND POST OCCUPANCY EVALUATION

If the original intention to evaluate all the houses using EcoHomes (Ref 8.2) had been followed through, then the houses could have been compared with each other and proposals measured against a variety of targets.

There were no resources to fund such an assessment for all of the houses and after the event some architects suggested that this was an opportunity lost. In the end, some did manage to secure resources to finance input in this respect from environmental services consultants whilst others did not.

Monitoring and post occupancy evaluation were highlighted by the architects as being critical in terms of making the paradigm shifts necessary to achieve The Scottish Government's targets on climate change mitigation and reduction in carbon emissions. Otherwise can we ever know which systems work best? Most of the arguments on the relative merits of a minimalist approach versus active energy solutions remain highly subjective. The Expo could provide an opportunity for direct comparisons of different systems/system types on one site.

POSITIVE EXPERIENCE

There are those who would argue that beyond aesthetics, the first Scottish Housing Expo achieved very little. For others it achieved much. One of the most important things that it did accomplish was that people started talking about architecture, design and place.
In addition, if one takes the time to read through the case studies in Chapter 6, it becomes clear that every house retained its signature features. There was a lot of discussion about breathing structures and moisture migration on the one hand and fully sealed mechanically ventilated homes on the other. What was perhaps less obvious to visitors was the innovative use of materials which were not visible in the completed construction. In fact more of the houses use natural (wood-fibre, cellulose, wool) insulation than use conventional systems such as rock or mineral wool and those who did opt for conventional materials, often used recycled products.

Due to the deletion of the site-wide district heating plant, many of the dwellings which had not costed-in a conventional system elected for the cheapest option – condensing gas combi-boilers – but 12 houses have air source heat pumps, 4 have woodburning stoves due to minimal heating requirements, and 4 have solar thermal heating and The Apartments on Plot 8 have a biomass (wood chip) group heating system (Ref 8.3).

FIGURE 8.7

GREEN JOBS

The Expo also explored opportunities for manufacturing products from home grown resources. As a result, two strong ideas have emerged, but this could lead to more projects coming to fruition. The two possible projects are outlined below.

Massive timber construction

Prior to the economic downturn, in association with the Forestry Commission Scotland and the Centre for Timber Engineering at Napier University, a local Highland timber product manufacturer had expressed an interest in setting up a plant to develop cross-laminated timber panels from Scottish grown timber. Fast growing Sitka spruce is ideally suited for this purpose as it has inadequate structural strength to be used in construction on its own, but if cross-laminated in layers, its strength is greatly enhanced. Although it was not possible in the end to manufacture locally, the Expo did test cross-laminated and other massive timber systems and further investigative work is now underway as a result of the showcasing at the Expo of this construction approach.

A Scottish Passive House

One team succeeded in producing and delivering a Scottish Passive House, which had no conventional heating system and a design that will achieve energy savings in the region of 80% over current Building Standards. In achieving this, the designers managed to hold on to increased insulation, design for high levels of air-tightness, the mechanical ventilation system, the high spec external windows and doors and even the tiled floor finish, specified to attenuate solar gains on the ground floor. This team was able to convince the developer that all of these elements worked in harmony as part of the whole house concept and to remove a single element or to reduce its specification would have meant the whole idea of a house without a conventional heating system could not be realised. These units had to be delivered for a similar budget to the others across the site, and so it was inevitable that some of the original features had to be deleted. Features removed included reclaimed stone cladding, internal finishes, bespoke joinery elements, and removal of additional renewable technologies, some of which would have delivered a house that was very close to zero carbon in-use.

In the architect's view, the project that emerged from the process was an even more robust concept than had at first been understood.

Throughout the design, the delivery and the event itself, a good collaborative and fruitful relationship was developed with the HHA and the developer. The design/construction team has continued to work collaboratively since the Expo to develop the passive house as a model for low energy affordable housing across Scotland. Perhaps it is on-going work like this that will become the most important legacy of Scotland's Housing Expo 2010.

THERMAL MASS vs TIMBER FRAME
The challenge for another practice was to create a three-storey building of 'affordable housing' flats. The original design had been for private flats for sale, but they became part of the affordable element of the Expo. This meant significant re-design, as all of the rooms in the flats had to meet the housing association client's space standards.

The design uses commonly available materials and understood construction techniques to create a building that aims to perform 'passively' to reduce the reliance on energy consumption for heating the spaces. The building has a recycled brick façade. From a buildability aspect, the structure was changed from an entirely load-bearing masonry system to largely timber kit, with masonry retained only where required by Building Standards or for thermal mass in relation to environmental performance. This decision improved the delivery programme by increasing site quality control and providing greater flexibility in achieving high levels of thermal insulation.

FIGURE 8.8

The decision not to have a district-heating scheme, which was originally proposed to provide all heating and domestic hot water requirements for the entire Expo site, resulted in a rigorous re-evaluation of potential energy sources for the project. A number of alternative options were reviewed and analysed, from both the aspect of environmental performance and capital and running costs. In the end, the opportunity to demonstrate a single energy source for a group of dwellings, coupled with the associated low carbon emissions, was adopted, resulting in the installation a communal biomass boiler within the curtilage of this plot.

Most importantly, this practice was able to retain the principles established at the outset, in terms of both aesthetics and environmental performance. The design team believes that it has produced a more responsibly considered solution without detracting from the essence of the design. The project also retained a key element of the original design - a three storey recycled brick façade. The design team is now working with the client and contractor to develop the design for affordable apartment – living elsewhere.

FIGURE 8.9

RELOCATION, RELOCATION

Another project benefited from relocation. Originally designed for a plot on the Green, but allocated a different site altogether, this house had to be completely re-designed internally to function well on its new site. Initially this was disappointing for the designers, but on reflection, the re-designed building works better on the new site enjoying some of the best passive solar opportunities and the best views of all of the Expo houses.

The design supports a mainly passive approach, with roof, walls and floors insulated to a standard approximately 60% higher than the requirements of the 2007 Building Standards. The high performance windows and doors have been triple glazed and considerable care was taken in the detail design to ensure that the timber frame house is well draught proofed. Together with well-controlled ventilation, this allows the house to achieve further energy efficiency improvements. In addition, an air source heat pump, provides the main heating by producing around four times as much energy as it uses to heat the house. The design also has a wood burning stove, which provides an alternative in milder weather to maximise the efficiency of the system. Roof mounted solar thermal panels and a large hot water buffer storage tank provide the majority of the hot water and space heating requirements for much of the year.

This design team worked closely with the developer partner, in developing the detail design to ensure that it was practicable and affordable, while achieving the design standards sought. In the process, some of the construction methods changed, and while some compromise was necessary, this process of collaborative working benefited both the partners and the project.

The above demonstrate that despite difficult economic times and working within a contract type that was imposed on the architects, where they could have lost all control over their projects, by developing good working relationships with their contractors most architects retained the key aspects of their projects. In some cases they have gone on to research the possibilities of taking this work forward into the mainstream.

" In the process, some of the construction methods changed, and while some compromise was necessary, this process of collaborative working benefited both the partners and the project."

FIGURE 8.10

NEW MODEL REQUIRED

The experiences of the architects and contractors varied greatly, and the solution of a design and build approach was embraced by some better than others. In some ways it simplified things for the HHA, but it also added complication due to disharmony in some quarters, which had to be managed. Most architects involved agree that it was well worth doing, but the majority would like to see a different delivery model within realistic timescales in the event of a future Expo.

While it was felt that the Finnish model was not suited to our construction and health and safety models, one project was delivered in a manner very close to that of the Finnish Fairs. The Secret Garden on Plot 17 was the only project delivered by an independent architect/ developer team from the Isle of Skye. Interestingly, this project was completed first, in advance of all of the other plots, to an extremely high standard of finish, and attracted more sponsorship in the form of furniture, fixtures and fittings and flooring and paint finishes than any other house on the site. This may be because of the commitment of the architect and contractor, who were both able to focus solely on this project, or it may be that the sponsors, many of whom were based on Skye, were quick to grasp the potential marketing benefits of the Expo. It would be interesting to know how much of the success of this project was due to working as a developer/architect team to demonstrate that the solution to costs does not have to be provided by scale.

The other extreme has to be the house designed for, but not built on Plot 10. The Design Team felt that the process was hampered by an over-riding view that innovation costs more. In contrast they were of the view that innovative sustainable buildings can be delivered at the same price as standard approaches, but only if everyone is motivated, smart and creative. To that end the Design Team, which included two contractors, submitted a tender to build the project which was within budget.

However, the main contractor priced the house at a higher cost, although the price contained prelims which appeared inordinately high and remained unexplained. In addition, it was decided that there was no leeway to allow another contractor on site and in the end, the negotiations ran out of time. The team was left dissatisfied by the process and would have loved to have had the opportunity to deliver the project themselves. Had they been given this opportunity we could have begun to draw conclusions on the benefits or otherwise of adopting the Finnish model here in Scotland.

SHOULD IT BE DONE AGAIN?

Overwhelmingly the conclusion from post-Expo focus group meetings with the architects and others who visited the site in August 2010, was that there should be more Expos – in order not only to raise the bar again, but also to put into practice what was learned on delivering the first one. The Expo provided an opportunity to do what we needed to do: to demonstrate what can be done within costs. Most of the architects would participate again, but there was a clear call for the need for a framework agreement between architects and much more encouragement and opportunity for them to work together. They all felt that the timescale for this event had been too tight to resolve the design of the houses properly, and to reach the standard of finish that they had aspired to.

At a time of economic difficulty, the Expo gave so many practices much needed work, and particularly gave an opportunity to young architects and some of the smaller practices .

There was a strong sense that the problems arising from procurement can be tackled for future events. One architect observed that it was noticeable that the projects where the developer was building the house that they had been involved with from the outset, went relatively well because a two-way relationship of trust had already been established.

REVIEW

The Scottish Government is currently conducting a review of the Expo to evaluate the success of the project and to learn from the ideas and experiences of those who took part in its creation and who visited the event in August 2010. The review will take account of what is learnt from those consulted in developing ideas for holding similar events in Scotland in the future, which would build on the successes and achievements of the first Expo.

Lori McElroy
Kate Hendry
The Architects

REFERENCES AND ACKNOWLEDGEMENTS

EDITORS AND CO-ORDINATORS
Sust. Programme, A+DS

Kate Hendry
Lori McElroy
Graeme McKirdy

REFERENCES/BIBLIOGRAPHY
CHAPTER 1
1.1 Sust. – www.sust.org

1.2 Expo Board and Principal Partners
THE BOARD
Forestry Commission Scotland
The Highland Council
Highland Birchwoods
Highland Housing Alliance
Highlands and Islands Enterprise
Highland Opportunities Ltd
Inverness Architectural Association
Sust. Programme, Architecture +Design
Scotland
The Scottish Government

PRINCIPAL PARTNERS
Event Scotland
Forestry Commission Scotland
Highland Housing Alliance
Highlands and Islands Enterprise
Homes for Scotland
Inverness Common Good Fund
Sust. Programme, Architecture +Design
Scotland
The Highland Council
The Scottish Government

CHAPTER 2
2.1 Suomi Asuntomessut – www.
asuntomessut.fi/yleistieto/en_GB/general

CHAPTER 3

3.1 West 8 Waterfront – Borneo Sporenburg, Amsterdam – www.west8.nl/projects/urban_design/borneo_sporenburg

3.2 Ecohomes – www.breeam.org

3.3 Six Cities Design Festival – en.wikipedia.org/wiki/Six_Cities_Design_Festival

CHAPTER 5

5.1 Claystation – www.remodellingdesign.com

5.2 New Start Highland – www.newstarthighland.org

5.3 Edinburgh International Science Festival – www.sciencefestival.co.uk

5.4 The Highland Countryside Rangers – www.highland.gov.uk/leisureandtourism

5.5 Architecture and Design Scotland – www.ads.org.uk

5.6 Spaces of Labour – www.spacesoflabour.com

5.7 ANTA – www.anta.co.uk

5.8 Housing: Fresh Thinking New Ideas and Homes Fit for the 21st Century – www.scotland.gov.uk/Topics/Built-Environment/Housing/reform

CHAPTER 6

6.1 Hans Monderman – en.wikipedia.org/wiki/Hans_Monderman

6.2 Craigmillar Urban Design Framework: Planning Advice Note 83 – www.scotland.gov.uk/Publications/2008/11/10114526/9

6.3 JJI Joists by James Jones and Sons Ltd – www.jji-joists.co.uk/

CHAPTER 7

7.1 RIBA Plan of Work – www.architecture.com/Files/RIBAProfessionalServices/Practice/OutlinePlanofWork(revised).pdf

CHAPTER 8

8.1 Trombe Michel Wall – en.wikipedia.org/wiki/Trombe_wall

8.2 Ecohomes – www.breeam.org

8.3 Biomass Heating System – Highland Birchwoods – www.highlandbirchwoods.co.uk

ACKNOWLEDGEMENTS

RIAS

Wayne and Gerardine Hemingway

Pasi Heiskanen - Suomi Asuntomessut

EVENT TEAM

The Highland Council

The House Ambassadors

Cobbs

Dynam

999 Design

Smarts

ARCHITECTS/MASTERPLANNER

Cadell2

A+J Burridge

AIM Design

Andrew Black Design

Bracewell Stirling

Brennan and Wilson Architects

David Blaike Architects

David Somerville Architects

Graeme Massie Architects

Graham Mitchell Architects

HLM Architects

JM Architects

John Gilbert Architects

Joseph Thurrott Architects

Keppie design

Locate Architects

Malcolm Fraser Architects

McLean Architects

NORD

Oliver Chapman Architects

Richard Murphy Architects

Rural Design

Studio KAP Architects

The Highland Council

Trevor Black Architects

DEVELOPERS AND CONTRACTORS

Albyn Housing Society
Cairn Housing Association
Highland Housing Alliance
Tulloch Homes Express
Morrison Homes
Robertson Highland
William Gray Construction
O'Brien Homes
James MacQueen Building Contractor
GF Job

EXHIBITORS

A+DS/ Sust
Albyn Housing Society
ANTA
Cairn Housing Association
Claystation
Edinburgh Science Centre
Forestry Commission Scotland
Highland Birchwoods
Invisible Heating Systems
NHBC
New Start Highland
Registers of Scotland
RSPB
Russwood
Scottish Ecological Design Association
The Highland Council
The Scottish Passive House Centre
University of Strathclyde
Wood For Good

SPONSORS

CONSTRUCTION

Timber and Timber products

Anta
Caley Timber
Deeside Timberframe
Forestry Commission Scotland
Highland Birchwoods
MAKAR Ltd
Mayr Melnhof Holz
MGMTimber
Passive Wall
Russwood
Scotframe
Scottish Passive House Centre
UPM Tillhill

Aggregates/Quarry Products

Aggregate Industries
Leiths

Glass and Glazing Products

D&D Glazing
Dynamight
Nordan
Velfac
Velux

Roofing and waterproofing

AAC Waterproofing
CLM Roofing

Landscaping and gardens

A+D Sutherland
Highland Landscapes

Visualisation

Envision 3D Limited

Play Equipment

Timberplay

OTHER ORGANISATIONS

BLP (Building Defects Insurance)
Dunfermline Building Society
HSPC
NHBC
Premier Guarantee
Registers of Scotland
RSPB
Scottish Ecological Design Association

SPONSORS

INTERIORS

Timber and Timber Products	Cromartie Timber
	Gavin Macdonald Flooring
	Russwood
Furniture/ Interiors	The Byre
	Clo Surface Design
	Concept
	Craft House
	GOODD
	IKEA
	Ma Maison Ecossaise
	New Start Highland
	Realise-Furniture.co.uk
	Scottish Furniture Makers
Kitchens	Ashley Anne Kitchens
	IKEA
	Kaufmann
	Neff
Energy systems, bathrooms & plumbing	Bathstore
	Bonk & Co
	Cosmo Ceramics
	Ceramic Tile Distributors
	Ideal Standard
	Invisible Heating Systems
	Morsø
	Plumb Centre
	Porcelanosa
	Solus Ceramics
Lighting	Eden Illumination
	Moleta Munro
	Philips
	Trilight
Ironmongery and Interior Finishes	Allgood
	D-Line
	Earthborn Paints
	Fakro
	HIS
	Morton Young & Borland
	Skye Finishing Touches
	WA McGarrie

IMAGE CREDITS

CHAPTER ONE
Figure 1.1, 1.2, 1.5, 1.7, 1.8 – Kate Hendry

Figure 1.3, 1.4, 1.6 – Ewen Wetherspoon

CHAPTER TWO
Figure 2.1, 2.4, 2.6, 2.7 – Ian Baird

Figure 2.2 – Rufus Logan

Figure 2.3, 2.5, 2.8, 2.9, 2.10– Kate Hendry

CHAPTER THREE
Figure 3.1 –The Highland Council

Figure 3.2, 3.3, 3.4, 3.5, 3.6, 3.7, 3.8, 3.9, 3.10 – Cadell2

Figure 3.11, 3.12 – Alan Dimmick

CHAPTER FOUR
Figure 4.1, 4.2, 4.3, 4.4 , 4.5, 4.6 – The Highland Housing Alliance

CHAPTER FIVE
Figure 5.1, 5.12, 5.15, 5.16, 5.18, 5.19, 5.20 – Kate Hendry

Figure 5.2, 5.3, 5.4, 5.5, 5.6, 5.7, 5.8, 5.9 – Ewen Wetherspoon

Figure 5.10 – John Gilbert Architects

Figure 5.11, 5.13, 5.17 – Alan Dimmick

Figure 5.14 – Lynne Cox

CHAPTER SIX INTRODUCTION
Figure 6.1 – Kate Hendry

Figure 6.2, 6.3, 6.4, 6.5, 6.6, 6.7, 6.8, 6.10, 6.11, 6.13, 6.14, 6.15 – Cadell2

Figure 6.9 – Getty Images

Figure 6.12 – The Lighthouse Trust

Figure 6.16 – Ewen Wetherspoon

CHAPTER SIX CASE STUDIES
PLOT 1 STEALTH TERRACE
Figure 1, 3, 4, 5, 6 – Ewen Wetherspoon

Figure 2 – JM Architects

PLOT 2 THE STONE HOUSE
Figure 1, 2, 4, 6 – Ewen Wetherspoon

Figure 3, 5 – Kate Hendry

PLOT 3 THE SHED HOUSE
Figure 1, 2, 3, 4, 5 – Ewen Wetherspoon

PLOT 4.1 THE TIMBER HOUSE
Figure 1, 2, 4 – Ewen Wetherspoon

Figure 3 – Kate Hendry

Figure 5 – John Gilbert Architects

PLOT 4.2 THE HEALTHY HOUSE
Figure 1, 2, 3, 4, 5, 6 - Ewen Wetherspoon

PLOT 4.3 LIOS GORM (GREEN PLACE TO LIVE)
Figure 1 - Paul Zanre

Figure 2 – David Blakie Architects

Figure 3, 4, 5 – Ewen Wetherspoon

PLOT 5 THE CORNER HOUSE

Figure 1 – JM Architects

Figure 2, 3, 4, 5, 6 – Ewen Wetherspoon

PLOT 6 WOODROCK

Figure 1, 2, 3, 4, 5, 6 – Ewen Wetherspoon

PLOT 7 HOUSE NO 7

Figure 1 – Kate Hendry

Figure 2, 3, 4, 5, 6 – Ewen Wetherspoon

PLOT 8 THE APARTMENTS

Figure 1, 2, 5, 6 – Ewen Wetherspoon

Figure 3, 4 – Kate Hendry

PLOT 9 THREE ON NINE

Figure 1, 3, 4 – Ewen Wetherspoon

Figure 2 – Kate Hendry

PLOT 10 MASSIVE PASSIVE

Figure 1, 2, 3, 4 – Locate Architects

PLOT 11 THE PASSIVE HOUSE

Figure 1, 2, 3, 4, 5, 6 – Ewen Wetherspoon

PLOT 12 THE GEM

Figure 1, 3, 4, 5 – Ewen Wetherspoon

Figure 2 – Kate Hendry

PLOT 14 THE SKYLIGHT HOME

Figure 1, 3, 4, 5, 6 – Ewen Wetherspoon

Figure 2 – Kate Hendry

PLOT 15 THE MODULAR HOUSE

Figure 1, 4 – Ewen Wetherspoon

Figure 2 – Kate Hendry

Figure 3 – Bracewell Stirling Architects

PLOT 16 WHITE HOUSE

Figure 1, 2, 3, 4 – Graeme Massie Architects

PLOT 17 THE SECRET GARDEN

Figure 1 – Kate Hendry

Figure 2, 4, 5, 6 – Rural Design

Figure 3 – Ewen Wetherspoon

PLOT 18 THE WHOLE LIFE HOUSE

Figure 1, 4, 5, 6 – Ewen Wetherspoon

Figure 2, 3 – Nigel Rigden Photography

PLOT 19 TWIN PEAKS

Figure 1, 2, 3 – Ewen Wetherspoon

Figure 4, 5 – Kate Hendry

PLOT 20 PLOT 20

Figure 1, 2, 4 – Ewen Wetherspoon

Figure 3 – Kate Hendry

PLOT 21 BLACK HOUSE

Figure 1, 2 – Graeme Massie Architects

PLOT 22 HOUSE HS

Figure 1, 3 – Ewen Wetherspoon

Figure 2 – Kate Hendry

Figure 4 – Simon Leeman

PLOT 23 THE SKEWED HOUSE

Figure 1, 2, 3, 4, 5 – Ewen Wetherspoon

PLOT 24 RED HOMES

Figure 1, 3, 4 – Ewen Wetherspoon

Figure 2 – Paul Zanre

PLOT 25 THE FLOWER HOUSE

Figure 1, 2, 3, 4, 5, 6, 7 – Ewen Wetherspoon

PLOT 26 THE HARDCORE SOFTHOUSE

Figure 1, 5 – Studio KAP Architects

Figure 2, 3, 4 – Ewen Wetherspoon

PLOT 27 HOUSE NS

Figure 1 – Claire Logan

Figure 2, 3, 4 – Ewen Wetherspoon

PLOTS 1-27 – ALL ARCHITECTURAL
DRAWINGS SUPPLIED BY THE
ARCHITECTS

CHAPTER SEVEN

Figure 7.1, 7.4, 7.18, 7.19, 7.20, 7.21, 7.22, 7.24,
7.25, 7.26, 7.28 – Kate Hendry

Figure 7.2, 7.6 - Ewen Wetherspoon

Figure 7.3, 7.5, 7.7, 7.8, 7.9, 7.10, 7.11, 7.12,
7.13, 7.14, 7.15, 7.16, 7.17 – Cadell2

Figure 7.23 – JM Architects

Figure 7.27 – Paul Zanre

CHAPTER EIGHT

Figure 8.1, 8.8, 8.10 – Ewen Wetherspoon

Figure 8.2, 8.3, 8.4, 8.5, 8.6, 8.7, 8.9 –
Kate Hendry